BIG IDEAS
MATH®
Integrated Mathematics I

Student Journal

- Maintaining Mathematical Proficiency
- Exploration Journal
- Notetaking with Vocabulary
- Extra Practice

BIG IDEAS LEARNING®

Erie, Pennsylvania

Photo Credits

ISBN 13: 978-1-68033-052-6
ISBN 10: 1-68033-052-7

10 11 12 13 14   23 22 21 20 19

Contents

About the Student Journal x

Chapter 1   Solving Linear Equations

Maintaining Mathematical Proficiency 1

1.1   Solving Simple Equations

Exploration Journal 2

Notetaking with Vocabulary/Extra Practice 4

1.2   Solving Multi-Step Equations

Exploration Journal 7

Notetaking with Vocabulary/Extra Practice 9

1.3   Solving Equations with Variables on Both Sides

Exploration Journal 12

Notetaking with Vocabulary/Extra Practice 14

1.4   Solving Absolute Value Equations

Exploration Journal 17

Notetaking with Vocabulary/Extra Practice 19

1.5   Rewriting Equations and Formulas

Exploration Journal 22

Notetaking with Vocabulary/Extra Practice 24

Chapter 2   Solving Linear Inequalities

Maintaining Mathematical Proficiency 27

2.1   Writing and Graphing Inequalities

Exploration Journal 28

Notetaking with Vocabulary/Extra Practice 30

2.2   Solving Inequalities Using Addition or Subtraction

Exploration Journal 33

Notetaking with Vocabulary/Extra Practice 35

2.3   Solving Inequalities Using Multiplication or Division

Exploration Journal 38

Notetaking with Vocabulary/Extra Practice 40

2.4   Solving Multi-Step Inequalities

Exploration Journal 43

Notetaking with Vocabulary/Extra Practice 45

2.5   Solving Compound Inequalities

Exploration Journal 48

Notetaking with Vocabulary/Extra Practice 50

Contents

2.6 Solving Absolute Value Inequalities

Exploration Journal 53

Notetaking with Vocabulary/Extra Practice 55

Chapter 3 Graphing Linear Functions

Maintaining Mathematical Proficiency 58

3.1 Functions

Exploration Journal 59

Notetaking with Vocabulary/Extra Practice 61

3.2 Linear Functions

Exploration Journal 64

Notetaking with Vocabulary/Extra Practice 66

3.3 Function Notation

Exploration Journal 69

Notetaking with Vocabulary/Extra Practice 71

3.4 Graphing Linear Equations in Standard Form

Exploration Journal 74

Notetaking with Vocabulary/Extra Practice 76

3.5 Graphing Linear Equations in Slope-Intercept Form

Exploration Journal 79

Notetaking with Vocabulary/Extra Practice 81

3.6 Transformations of Graphs of Linear Functions

Exploration Journal 84

Notetaking with Vocabulary/Extra Practice 86

Chapter 4 Writing Linear Functions

Maintaining Mathematical Proficiency 90

4.1 Writing Equations in Slope-Intercept Form

Exploration Journal 91

Notetaking with Vocabulary/Extra Practice 93

4.2 Writing Equations in Point-Slope Form

Exploration Journal 96

Notetaking with Vocabulary/Extra Practice 98

4.3 Writing Equations of Parallel and Perpendicular Lines

Exploration Journal 101

Notetaking with Vocabulary/Extra Practice 103

Contents

4.4 **Scatter Plots and Lines of Fit**

Exploration Journal 106

Notetaking with Vocabulary/Extra Practice 108

4.5 **Analyzing Lines of Fit**

Exploration Journal 111

Notetaking with Vocabulary/Extra Practice 113

4.6 **Arithmetic Sequences**

Exploration Journal 116

Notetaking with Vocabulary/Extra Practice 118

Chapter 5 **Solving Systems of Linear Equations**

Maintaining Mathematical Proficiency 121

5.1 **Solving Systems of Linear Equations by Graphing**

Exploration Journal 122

Notetaking with Vocabulary/Extra Practice 124

5.2 **Solving Systems of Linear Equations by Substitution**

Exploration Journal 127

Notetaking with Vocabulary/Extra Practice 129

5.3 **Solving Systems of Linear Equations by Elimination**

Exploration Journal 132

Notetaking with Vocabulary/Extra Practice 134

5.4 **Solving Special Systems of Linear Equations**

Exploration Journal 137

Notetaking with Vocabulary/Extra Practice 139

5.5 **Solving Equations by Graphing**

Exploration Journal 142

Notetaking with Vocabulary/Extra Practice 144

5.6 **Graphing Linear Inequalities in Two Variables**

Exploration Journal 147

Notetaking with Vocabulary/Extra Practice 149

5.7 **Systems of Linear Inequalities**

Exploration Journal 152

Notetaking with Vocabulary/Extra Practice 154

Chapter 6 **Exponential Functions and Sequences**

Maintaining Mathematical Proficiency 157

6.1 **Exponential Functions**

Exploration Journal 158

Notetaking with Vocabulary/Extra Practice 160

Contents

6.2 Exponential Growth and Decay

Exploration Journal 163

Notetaking with Vocabulary/Extra Practice 165

6.3 Comparing Linear and Exponential Functions

Exploration Journal 168

Notetaking with Vocabulary/Extra Practice 170

6.4 Solving Exponential Equations

Exploration Journal 173

Notetaking with Vocabulary/Extra Practice 175

6.5 Geometric Sequences

Exploration Journal 178

Notetaking with Vocabulary/Extra Practice 180

6.6 Recursively Defined Sequences

Exploration Journal 183

Notetaking with Vocabulary/Extra Practice 185

Chapter 7 Data Analysis and Displays

Maintaining Mathematical Proficiency 188

7.1 Measures of Center and Variation

Exploration Journal 189

Notetaking with Vocabulary/Extra Practice 191

7.2 Box-and-Whisker Plots

Exploration Journal 195

Notetaking with Vocabulary/Extra Practice 197

7.3 Shapes of Distributions

Exploration Journal 200

Notetaking with Vocabulary/Extra Practice 202

7.4 Two-Way Tables

Exploration Journal 205

Notetaking with Vocabulary/Extra Practice 207

7.5 Choosing a Data Display

Exploration Journal 210

Notetaking with Vocabulary/Extra Practice 212

Contents

Chapter 8   **Basics of Geometry**

Maintaining Mathematical Proficiency 215

8.1   **Points, Lines, and Planes**

Exploration Journal 216

Notetaking with Vocabulary/Extra Practice...218

8.2   **Measuring and Constructing Segments**

Exploration Journal 221

Notetaking with Vocabulary/Extra Practice...223

8.3   **Using Midpoint and Distance Formulas**

Exploration Journal 226

Notetaking with Vocabulary/Extra Practice...228

8.4   **Perimeter and Area in the Coordinate Plane**

Exploration Journal 231

Notetaking with Vocabulary/Extra Practice...233

8.5   **Measuring and Constructing Angles**

Exploration Journal 236

Notetaking with Vocabulary/Extra Practice...238

8.6   **Describing Pairs of Angles**

Exploration Journal 241

Notetaking with Vocabulary/Extra Practice...243

Chapter 9   **Reasoning and Proofs**

Maintaining Mathematical Proficiency 246

9.1   **Conditional Statements**

Exploration Journal 247

Notetaking with Vocabulary/Extra Practice...249

9.2   **Inductive and Deductive Reasoning**

Exploration Journal 253

Notetaking with Vocabulary/Extra Practice...255

9.3   **Postulates and Diagrams**

Exploration Journal 258

Notetaking with Vocabulary/Extra Practice...260

9.4   **Proving Statements about Segments and Angles**

Exploration Journal 263

Notetaking with Vocabulary/Extra Practice...265

Contents

9.5   **Proving Geometric Relationships**

Exploration Journal 269

Notetaking with Vocabulary/Extra Practice 271

Chapter 10   **Parallel and Perpendicular Lines**

Maintaining Mathematical Proficiency 274

10.1   **Pairs of Lines and Angles**

Exploration Journal 275

Notetaking with Vocabulary/Extra Practice 277

10.2   **Parallel Lines and Transversals**

Exploration Journal 281

Notetaking with Vocabulary/Extra Practice 283

10.3   **Proofs with Parallel Lines**

Exploration Journal 286

Notetaking with Vocabulary/Extra Practice 288

10.4   **Proofs with Perpendicular Lines**

Exploration Journal 291

Notetaking with Vocabulary/Extra Practice 293

10.5   **Using Parallel and Perpendicular Lines**

Exploration Journal 296

Notetaking with Vocabulary/Extra Practice 298

Chapter 11   **Transformations**

Maintaining Mathematical Proficiency 301

11.1   **Translations**

Exploration Journal 302

Notetaking with Vocabulary/Extra Practice 304

11.2   **Reflections**

Exploration Journal 307

Notetaking with Vocabulary/Extra Practice 309

11.3   **Rotations**

Exploration Journal 312

Notetaking with Vocabulary/Extra Practice 314

11.4   **Congruence and Transformations**

Exploration Journal 317

Notetaking with Vocabulary/Extra Practice 319

Contents

Chapter 12 **Congruent Triangles**

Maintaining Mathematical Proficiency 322

12.1 **Angles of Triangles**

Exploration Journal 323

Notetaking with Vocabulary/Extra Practice 325

12.2 **Congruent Polygons**

Exploration Journal 328

Notetaking with Vocabulary/Extra Practice 330

12.3 **Proving Triangle Congruence by SAS**

Exploration Journal 333

Notetaking with Vocabulary/Extra Practice 335

12.4 **Equilateral and Isosceles Triangles**

Exploration Journal 338

Notetaking with Vocabulary/Extra Practice 340

12.5 **Proving Triangle Congruence by SSS**

Exploration Journal 343

Notetaking with Vocabulary/Extra Practice 345

12.6 **Proving Triangle Congruence by ASA and AAS**

Exploration Journal 348

Notetaking with Vocabulary/Extra Practice 350

12.7 **Using Congruent Triangles**

Exploration Journal 353

Notetaking with Vocabulary/Extra Practice 355

12.8 **Coordinate Proofs**

Exploration Journal 358

Notetaking with Vocabulary/Extra Practice 360

About the Student Journal

Maintaining Mathematical Proficiency

The Maintaining Mathematical Proficiency corresponds to the Pupil Edition Chapter Opener. Here you have the opportunity to practice prior skills necessary to move forward.

Exploration Journal

The Exploration pages correspond to the Explorations and accompanying exercises in the Pupil Edition. Here you have room to show your work and record your answers.

Notetaking with Vocabulary

This student-friendly notetaking component is designed to be a reference for key vocabulary, properties, and core concepts from the lesson. There is room to add definitions in your words and take notes about the core concepts.

Extra Practice

Each section of the Pupil Edition has an additional Practice with room for you to show your work and record your answers.

Maintaining Mathematical Proficiency

Add or subtract.

1. $-1 + (-3)$ 2. $0 + (-12)$ 3. $5 - (-2)$ 4. $-4 - 7$

5. Find two pairs of integers whose sum is -6.

6. In a city, the record monthly high temperature for March is $56°F$. The record monthly low temperature for March is $-4°F$. What is the range of temperatures for the month of March?

Multiply or divide.

7. $-2(13)$ 8. $-8 \cdot (-5)$ 9. $\dfrac{14}{2}$ 10. $-30 \div (-3)$

11. Find two pairs of integers whose product is -20.

12. A football team loses 3 yards in 3 consecutive plays. What is the total yardage gained?

Name _____ Date _____

1.1 Solving Simple Equations
For use with Exploration 1.1

Essential Question How can you use simple equations to solve real-life problems?

1 EXPLORATION: Measuring Angles

Go to *BigIdeasMath.com* for an interactive tool to investigate this exploration.

Work with a partner. Use a protractor to measure the angles of each quadrilateral. Complete the table to organize your results. (The notation $m\angle A$ denotes the measure of angle A.) How precise are your measurements?

a. 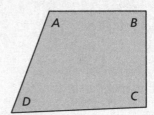 b. 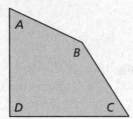 c.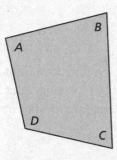

Quadrilateral	$m\angle A$ (degrees)	$m\angle B$ (degrees)	$m\angle C$ (degrees)	$m\angle D$ (degrees)	$m\angle A + m\angle B + m\angle C + m\angle D$
a.					
b.					
c.					

2 EXPLORATION: Making a Conjecture

Go to *BigIdeasMath.com* for an interactive tool to investigate this exploration.

Work with a partner. Use the completed table in Exploration 1 to write a conjecture about the sum of the angle measures of a quadrilateral. Draw three quadrilaterals that are different from those in Exploration 1 and use them to justify your conjecture.

Name_____ Date_____

1.1 **Solving Simple Equations** (continued)

---

3 **EXPLORATION:** Applying Your Conjecture

Go to *BigIdeasMath.com* for an interactive tool to investigate this exploration.

Work with a partner. Use the conjecture you wrote in Exploration 2 to write an equation for each quadrilateral. Then solve the equation to find the value of *x*. Use a protractor to check the reasonableness of your answer.

a.
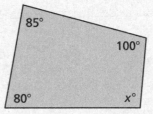

b.
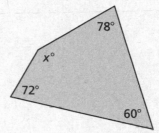

c.
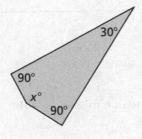

Communicate Your Answer

4. How can you use simple equations to solve real-life problems?

5. Draw your own quadrilateral and cut it out. Tear off the four corners of the quadrilateral and rearrange them to affirm the conjecture you wrote in Exploration 2. Explain how this affirms the conjecture.

1.1 Notetaking with Vocabulary
For use after Lesson 1.1

In your own words, write the meaning of each vocabulary term.

conjecture

rule

theorem

equation

linear equation in one variable

solution

inverse operations

equivalent equations

Core Concepts

Addition Property of Equality

Let a, b, and c be real numbers.

If $a = b$, then $a + c = b + c$.

Notes:

Subtraction Property of Equality

Let a, b, and c be real numbers.

If $a = b$, then $a - c = b - c$.

Notes:

1.1 **Notetaking with Vocabulary** (continued)

Substitution Property of Equality

Let a, b, and c be real numbers.

If $a = b$, then a can be substituted for b (or b for a) in any equation or expression.

Notes:

Multiplication Property of Equality

Let a, b, and c be real numbers.

If $a = b$, then $a \bullet c = b \bullet c$, $c \neq 0$.

Notes:

Division Property of Equality

Let a, b, and c be real numbers.

If $a = b$, then $\dfrac{a}{c} = \dfrac{b}{c}$, $c \neq 0$.

Notes:

Four Step Approach to Problem Solving

1. **Understand the Problem** What is the unknown? What information is being given? What is being asked?

2. **Make a Plan** This plan might involve one or more of the problem-solving strategies shown on the following page.

3. **Solve the Problem** Carry out your plan. Check that each step is correct.

4. **Look Back** Examine your solution. Check that your solution makes sense in the original statement of the problem.

Notes:

1.1 Notetaking with Vocabulary (continued)

Common Problem-Solving Strategies

Use a verbal model.	Guess, check, and revise.
Draw a diagram.	Sketch a graph or number line.
Write an equation.	Make a table.
Look for a pattern.	Make a list.
Work backward.	Break the problem into parts.

Notes:

Extra Practice

In Exercises 1–9, solve the equation. Justify each step. Check your solution.

1. $w + 4 = 16$

2. $x + 7 = -12$

3. $-15 + w = 6$

4. $z - 5 = 8$

5. $-2 = y - 9$

6. $7q = 35$

7. $4b = -52$

8. $3 = \dfrac{q}{11}$

9. $\dfrac{n}{-2} = -15$

10. A coupon subtracts $17.95 from the price p of a pair of headphones. You pay $71.80 for the headphones after using the coupon. Write and solve an equation to find the original price of the headphones.

11. After a party, you have $\dfrac{2}{5}$ of the brownies you made left over. There are 16 brownies left. How many brownies did you make for the party?

1.2 Solving Multi-Step Equations
For use with Exploration 1.2

Essential Question How can you use multi-step equations to solve real-life problems?

1 EXPLORATION: Solving for the Angle Measures of a Polygon

Go to *BigIdeasMath.com* for an interactive tool to investigate this exploration.

Work with a partner. The sum S of the angle measures of a polygon with n sides can be found using the formula $S = 180(n - 2)$. Write and solve an equation to find each value of x. Justify the steps in your solution. Then find the angle measures of each polygon. How can you check the reasonableness of your answers?

a.
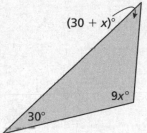

b.
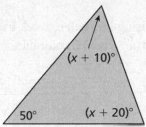

c.
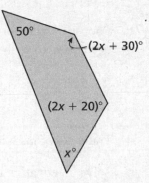

d.
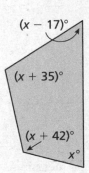

e.
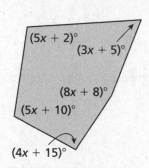

f.
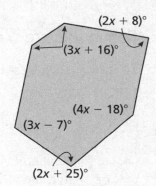

1.2 Solving Multi-Step Equations (continued)

2 EXPLORATION: Writing a Multi-Step Equation

Go to *BigIdeasMath.com* for an interactive tool to investigate this exploration.

Work with a partner.

  a. Draw an irregular polygon.

  b. Measure the angles of the polygon. Record the measurements on a separate sheet of paper.

  c. Choose a value for x. Then, using this value, work backward to assign a variable expression to each angle measure, as in Exploration 1.

  d. Trade polygons with your partner.

  e. Solve an equation to find the angle measures of the polygon your partner drew. Do your answers seem reasonable? Explain.

Communicate Your Answer

  3. How can you use multi-step equations to solve real-life problems?

  4. In Exploration 1, you were given the formula for the sum S of the angle measures of a polygon with n sides. Explain why this formula works.

  5. The sum of the angle measures of a polygon is 1080°. How many sides does the polygon have? Explain how you found your answer.

Name_____ Date_____

1.2 Notetaking with Vocabulary
For use after Lesson 1.2

In your own words, write the meaning of each vocabulary term.

inverse operations

mean

Core Concepts

Solving Multi-Step Equations

To solve a multi-step equation, simplify each side of the equation, if necessary. Then use inverse operations to isolate the variable.

Notes:

1.2 **Notetaking with Vocabulary** (continued)

Extra Practice

In Exercises 1–14, solve the equation. Check your solution.

1. $3x + 4 = 19$

2. $5z - 13 = -3$

3. $17 = z - (-9)$

4. $15 = 2 + 4 - d$

5. $\dfrac{f}{4} - 5 = -9$

6. $\dfrac{q + (-5)}{3} = 8$

7. $5x + 3x = 28$

8. $5z - 2z - 4 = -7$

9. $12x + 4 + 2x = 39$

10. $9z - 5 - 4z = -5$

1.2 Notetaking with Vocabulary (continued)

11. $3(z + 7) = 21$

12. $-4(z - 12) = 42$

13. $33 = 12r - 3(9 - r)$

14. $7 + 3(2g - 6) = -29$

15. You can represent an odd integer with the expression $2n + 1$, where n is any integer. Write and solve an equation to find three consecutive odd integers that have a sum of 63.

16. One angle of a triangle has a measure of $66°$. The measure of the third angle is $57°$ more than $\frac{1}{2}$ the measure of the second angle. The sum of the angle measures of a triangle is $180°$. What is the measure of the second angle? What is the measure of the third angle?

17. Your cousin is 8 years older than your brother. Three years ago, your cousin was twice as old as your brother. How old is your cousin now? How old is your brother now?

Name _____ Date _____

1.3 Solving Equations with Variables on Both Sides
For use with Exploration 1.3

Essential Question How can you solve an equation that has variables on both sides?

1 EXPLORATION: Perimeter

Work with a partner. The two polygons have the same perimeter. Use this information to write and solve an equation involving x. Explain the process you used to find the solution. Then find the perimeter of each polygon.

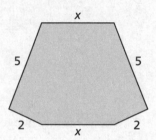
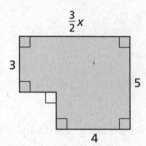

2 EXPLORATION: Perimeter and Area

Work with a partner.

• Each figure has the unusual property that the value of its perimeter (in feet) is equal to the value of its area (in square feet). Use this information to write an equation for each figure.

• Solve each equation for x. Explain the process you used to find the solution.

• Find the perimeter and area of each figure.

1.3 **Solving Equations with Variables on Both Sides** (continued)

---

2 **EXPLORATION:** Perimeter and Area (continued)

a.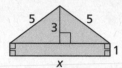

b.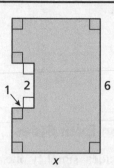

c.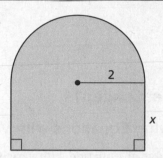

Communicate Your Answer

3. How can you solve an equation that has variables on both sides?

4. Write three equations that have the variable *x* on both sides. The equations should be different from those you wrote in Explorations 1 and 2. Have your partner solve the equations.

1.3 Notetaking with Vocabulary
For use after Lesson 1.3

In your own words, write the meaning of each vocabulary term.

identity

Core Concepts

Solving Equations with Variables on Both Sides

To solve an equation with variables on both sides, simplify one or both sides of the equation, if necessary. Then use inverse operations to collect the variable terms on one side, collect the constant terms on the other side, and isolate the variable.

Notes:

Special Solutions of Linear Equations

Equations do not always have one solution. An equation that is true for all values of the variable is an **identity** and has *infinitely many solutions*. An equation that is not true for any value of the variable has *no solution*.

Notes:

1.3 Notetaking with Vocabulary (continued)

Steps for Solving Linear Equations

Here are several steps you can use to solve a linear equation. Depending on the equation, you may not need to use some steps.

Step 1 Use the Distributive Property to remove any grouping symbols.

Step 2 Simplify the expression on each side of the equation.

Step 3 Collect the variable terms on one side of the equation and the constant terms on the other side.

Step 4 Isolate the variable.

Step 5 Check your solution.

Notes:

Extra Practice

In Exercises 1–10, solve the equation. Check your solution.

1. $12 - 3x = -6x$

2. $7 - 5z = 17 + 5z$

3. $3k + 45 = 8k + 25$

4. $\frac{3}{4}(48 - 16x) = 4(4 + 2x)$

5. $5q + 6 = 2q - 2 + q$

6. $8 + 6x - 10x = 16 - 8x$

1.3 **Notetaking with Vocabulary** (continued)

7. $6a - 4 = 3a + 5$

8. $2(4b - 6) = 4(3b - 7)$

9. $8(2r - 3) - r = 3(3r + 2)$

10. $3x - 8(2x + 3) = -6(2x + 5)$

In Exercises 11–14, solve the equation. Determine whether the equation has *one solution*, *no solution*, or *infinitely many solutions*.

11. $6(4s + 12) = 8(3s - 14)$

12. $16f + 24 = 8(2f + 3)$

13. $\frac{1}{2}(10 + 12n) = \frac{1}{3}(15n + 15)$

14. $\frac{2}{3}(6j + 9) = 3j + 7$

15. The value of the surface area of the rectangular prism is equal to the value of the volume of the rectangular prism. Write and solve an equation to find the value of x.

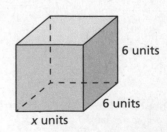

6 units

6 units

x units

1.4 Solving Absolute Value Equations
For use with Exploration 1.4

Essential Question   How can you solve an absolute value equation?

> **1** **EXPLORATION:** Solving an Absolute Value Equation Algebraically

Work with a partner. Consider the absolute value equation $|x + 2| = 3$.

   a. Describe the values of $x + 2$ that make the equation true. Use your description to write two linear equations that represent the solutions of the absolute value equation.

   b. Use the linear equations you wrote in part (a) to find the solutions of the absolute value equation.

   c. How can you use linear equations to solve an absolute value equation?

> **2** **EXPLORATION:** Solving an Absolute Value Equation Graphically

Go to *BigIdeasMath.com* **for an interactive tool to investigate this exploration.**

Work with a partner. Consider the absolute value equation $|x + 2| = 3$.

   a. On a real number line, locate the point for which $x + 2 = 0$.

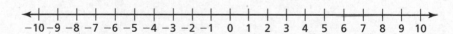

   b. Locate the points that are 3 units from the point you found in part (a). What do you notice about those points?

   c. How can you use a number line to solve an absolute value equation?

1.4 **Solving Absolute Value Equations** (continued)

3 **EXPLORATION: Solving an Absolute Value Equation Numerically**

Go to *BigIdeasMath.com* for an interactive tool to investigate this exploration.

Work with a partner. Consider the absolute value equation $|x + 2| = 3$.

a. Use a spreadsheet, as shown,
to solve the absolute value equation.

	A	B
1	**x**	**|x + 2|**
2	-6	4
3	-5	
4	-4	
5	-3	
6	-2	
7	-1	
8	0	
9	1	
10	2	

abs(A2 + 2)

b. Compare the solutions you found using
the spreadsheet with those you found
in Explorations 1 and 2. What do
you notice?

c. How can you use a spreadsheet to
solve an absolute value equation?

Communicate Your Answer

4. How can you solve an absolute value equation?

5. What do you like or dislike about the algebraic, graphical, and numerical methods
for solving an absolute value equation? Give reasons for your answers.

Name_____ Date_____

1.4 Notetaking with Vocabulary
For use after Lesson 1.4

In your own words, write the meaning of each vocabulary term.

absolute value equation

extraneous solution

Core Concepts

Properties of Absolute Value

Let a and b be real numbers. Then the following properties are true.

1. $|a| \geq 0$

2. $|-a| = |a|$

3. $|ab| = |a||b|$

4. $\left|\dfrac{a}{b}\right| = \dfrac{|a|}{|b|}, b \neq 0$

Notes:

1.4 **Notetaking with Vocabulary (continued)**

Solving Absolute Value Equations

To solve $|ax + b| = c$ when $c \geq 0$, solve the related linear equations

$$ax + b = c \quad or \quad ax + b = -c.$$

When $c < 0$, the absolute value equation $|ax + b| = c$ has no solution because absolute value always indicates a number that is not negative.

Notes:

Solving Equations with Two Absolute Values

To solve $|ax + b| = |cx + d|$, solve the related linear equations

$$ax + b = cx + d \quad or \quad ax + b = -(cx + d).$$

Notes:

Extra Practice

In Exercises 1–5, solve the equation. Graph the solution(s), if possible.

1. $|3x + 12| = 0$

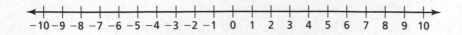

1.4 **Notetaking with Vocabulary** (continued)

2. $|y + 2| = 8$

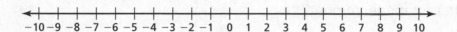

3. $-4|7 - 6k| = 14$

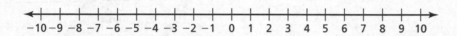

4. $\left|\dfrac{d}{3}\right| = 3$

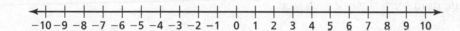

5. $3|2x + 5| + 10 = 37$

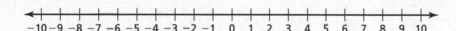

In Exercises 6–9, solve the equation. Check your solutions.

6. $|20x| = |4x + 16|$

7. $|p + 4| = |p - 2|$

8. $|4q + 9| = |2q - 1|$

9. $|2x - 7| = |2x + 9|$

1.5 Rewriting Equations and Formulas

For use with Exploration 1.5

Essential Question How can you use a formula for one measurement to write a formula for a different measurement?

1 EXPLORATION: Using an Area Formula

Work with a partner.

a. Write a formula for the area A of a parallelogram.

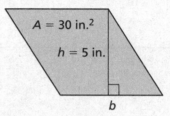

$A = 30\ \text{in.}^2$

$h = 5\ \text{in.}$

b

b. Substitute the given values into the formula. Then solve the equation for b. Justify each step.

c. Solve the formula in part (a) for b without first substituting values into the formula. Justify each step.

d. Compare how you solved the equations in parts (b) and (c). How are the processes similar? How are they different?

1.5 Rewriting Equations and Formulas (continued)

2 EXPLORATION: Using Area, Circumference, and Volume Formulas

Work with a partner. Write the indicated formula for each figure. Then write a new formula by solving for the variable whose value is not given. Use the new formula to find the value of the variable.

a. Area A of a trapezoid

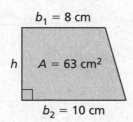

$b_1 = 8$ cm

h $A = 63$ cm^2

$b_2 = 10$ cm

b. Circumference C of a circle

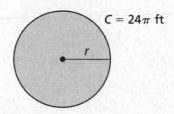

$C = 24\pi$ ft

r

c. Volume V of a rectangular prism

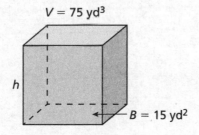

$V = 75$ yd^3

h

$B = 15$ yd^2

d. Volume V of a cone

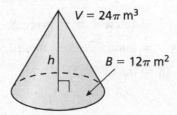

$V = 24\pi$ m^3

h $B = 12\pi$ m^2

Communicate Your Answer

3. How can you use a formula for one measurement to write a formula for a different measurement? Give an example that is different from those given in Explorations 1 and 2.

Name _____ Date _____

Notetaking with Vocabulary
For use after Lesson 1.5

In your own words, write the meaning of each vocabulary term.

literal equation

formula

Core Concepts

Common Formulas

Temperature	F = degrees Fahrenheit, C = degrees Celsius

$$C = \tfrac{5}{9}(F - 32)$$

Simple Interest I = interest, P = principal,

r = annual interest rate (decimal form),

t = time (years)

$$I = Prt$$

Distance d = distance traveled, r = rate, t = time

$$d = rt$$

Notes:

Name_____ Date_____

Notetaking with Vocabulary (continued)

Extra Practice

In Exercises 1–6, solve the literal equation for _y_.

1. $y - 2x = 15$

2. $4x + y = 2$

3. $5x - 2 = 8 + 5y$

4. $y + x = 11$

5. $3x - y = -4$

6. $3x + 1 = 7 - 4y$

In Exercises 7–12, solve the literal equation for _x_.

7. $y = 10x - 4x$

8. $q = 3x + 9xz$

9. $r = 4 + 7x - sx$

10. $y + 4x = 10x - 6$

11. $4g + r = 2r - 2x$

12. $3z + 8 = 12 + 3x - z$

In Exercises 13–16, solve the formula for the indicated variable.

13. Area of a triangle: $A = \frac{1}{2}bh$; Solve for b.

14. Volume of a cone: $V = \frac{1}{3}\pi r^2 h$; Solve for h.

1.5 **Notetaking with Vocabulary** (continued)

15. Ohm's Law: $I = \dfrac{V}{R}$; Solve for R.

16. Ideal Gas Law: $PV = nRT$; Solve for R.

17. The amount A of money in an account after simple interest has been earned is given by the formula $A = P + Prt$ where P is the principal, r is the annual interest rate in decimal form, and t is the time in years.

   a. Solve the formula for r.

   b. The amount of money in an account after interest has been earned is $1080, the principal is $1000, and the time is 2 years. What is the annual interest rate?

   c. Solve the formula for P.

Chapter 2 Maintaining Mathematical Proficiency

Graph the number.

1. $|-2|$

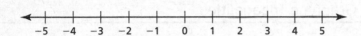

2. $-3 + |-3|$

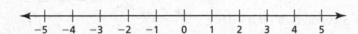

3. $-1 - |-4|$

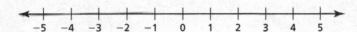

4. $2 + |2|$

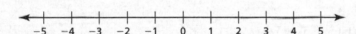

Complete the statement with $<$, $>$, or $=$.

5. 6 _____ 5

6. -2 _____ 3

7. -4 _____ -7

8. -8 _____ -5

9. $|-5|$ _____ 5

10. -7 _____ $|-6|$

11. A number a is to the right of a number b on the number line. Which is greater, $-a$ or $-b$?

12. A number a is to the left of a number b on the number line. Which is greater, $|-a|$ or $|-b|$?

2.1 Writing and Graphing Inequalities
For use with Exploration 2.1

Essential Question How can you use an inequality to describe a real-life statement?

1 EXPLORATION: Writing and Graphing Inequalities

Go to *BigIdeasMath.com* for an interactive tool to investigate this exploration.

Work with a partner. Write an inequality for each statement. Then sketch the graph of the numbers that make each inequality true.

a. **Statement** The temperature t in Sweden is at least $-10°C$.

Inequality

Graph
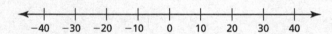

b. **Statement** The elevation e of Alabama is at most 2407 feet.

Inequality

Graph
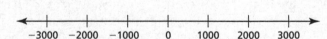

2 EXPLORATION: Writing Inequalities

Work with a partner. Write an inequality for each graph. Then, in words, describe all the values of x that make each inequality true.

a.
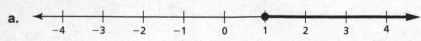

2.1 **Writing and Graphing Inequalities** (continued)

2 **EXPLORATION:** Writing Inequalities (continued)

b.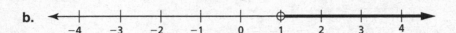

c.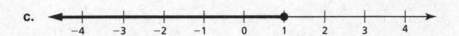

d.

Communicate Your Answer

3. How can you use an inequality to describe a real-life statement?

4. Write a real-life statement that involves each inequality.

   a. $x < 3.5$ **b.** $x \leq 6$

   c. $x > -2$ **d.** $x \geq 10$

2.1 Notetaking with Vocabulary
For use after Lesson 2.1

In your own words, write the meaning of each vocabulary term.

inequality

solution of an inequality

solution set

graph of an inequality

Core Concepts

Representing Linear Inequalities

Words	Algebra	Graph
x is less than 2	$x < 2$	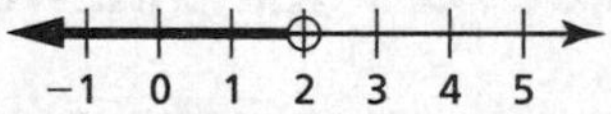
x is greater than 2	$x > 2$	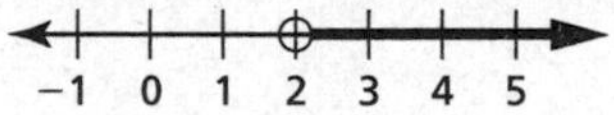
x is less than or equal to 2	$x \leq 2$	
x is greater than or equal to 2	$x \geq 2$	

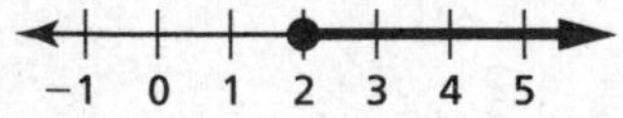

Notes:

2.1 **Notetaking with Vocabulary** (continued)

Extra Practice

In Exercises 1–4, write the sentence as an inequality.

1. Twelve is greater than or equal to five times a number n.

2. One-third of a number h is less than 15.

3. Seven is less than or equal to the difference of a number q and 6.

4. The sum of a number u and 14 is more than 6.

In Exercises 5 and 6, tell whether the value is a solution of the inequality.

5. $d - 7 < 12; d = 19$ 6. $9 \geq 3n + 6; n = 1$

In Exercises 7–10, graph the inequality.

7. $x \geq 3$

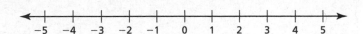

8. $x \leq 4$

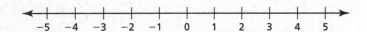

Integrated Mathematics I   **31**
Student Journal

2.1   **Notetaking with Vocabulary** (continued)

9. $x > -1$

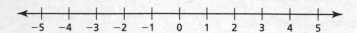

10. $x < 1$

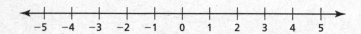

In Exercises 11–14, write an inequality that represents the graph.

11.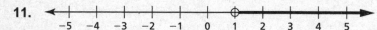

12.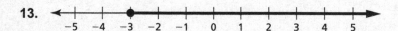

13.

14.

2.2 Solving Inequalities Using Addition or Subtraction
For use with Exploration 2.2

Essential Question How can you use addition or subtraction to solve an inequality?

---

1 EXPLORATION: Quarterback Passing Efficiency

Work with a partner. The National Collegiate Athletic Association (NCAA) uses the following formula to rank the passing efficiencies P of quarterbacks.

$$P = \frac{8.4Y + 100C + 330T - 200N}{A}$$

Y = total length of all completed passes (in **Y**ards) C = **C**ompleted passes

T = passes resulting in a **T**ouchdown N = i**N**tercepted passes

A = **A**ttempted passes M = inco**M**plete passes

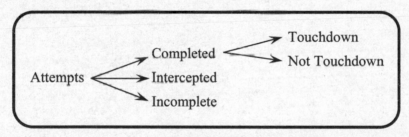

Determine whether each inequality must be true. Explain your reasoning.

a. $T < C$

b. $C + N \leq A$

c. $N < A$

d. $A - C \geq M$

2.2 Solving Inequalities Using Addition or Subtraction (continued)

---

2 EXPLORATION: Finding Solutions of Inequalities

Work with a partner. Use the passing efficiency formula to create a passing record that makes each inequality true. Record your results in the table. Then describe the values of P that make each inequality true.

	Attempts	Completions	Yards	Touchdowns	Interceptions
a.					
b.					
c.					

a. $P < 0$

b. $P + 100 \geq 250$

c. $P - 250 > -80$

Communicate Your Answer

3. How can you use addition or subtraction to solve an inequality?

4. Solve each inequality.

   a. $x + 3 < 4$ b. $x - 3 \geq 5$

   c. $4 > x - 2$ d. $-2 \leq x + 1$

Name_____ Date_____

2.2 Notetaking with Vocabulary
For use after Lesson 2.2

In your own words, write the meaning of each vocabulary term.

equivalent inequalities

Notes:

Core Concepts

Addition Property of Inequality

Words Adding the same number to each side of an inequality produces an equivalent inequality.

Numbers
$$-3 < 2 \qquad\qquad -3 \geq -10$$
$$\underline{+\,4 \quad +\,4} \qquad\qquad \underline{+\,3 \quad +\,3}$$
$$1 < 6 \qquad\qquad 0 \geq -7$$

Algebra If $a > b$, then $a + c > b + c$.   If $a \geq b$, then $a + c \geq b + c$.

If $a < b$, then $a + c < b + c$.   If $a \leq b$, then $a + c \leq b + c$.

Notes:

2.2 **Notetaking with Vocabulary** (continued)

Subtraction Property of Inequality

Words Subtracting the same number from each side of an inequality produces an
equivalent inequality.

Numbers $\begin{array}{r} -3 \le \ \ \ 1 \\ \underline{-5 \ \ \ -5} \\ -8 \le -4 \end{array}$ $\qquad$ $\begin{array}{r} 7 > -20 \\ \underline{-7 \ \ \ -7} \\ 0 > -27 \end{array}$

Algebra If $a > b$, then $a - c > b - c$. $\qquad$ If $a \ge b$, then $a - c \ge b - c$.

If $a < b$, then $a - c < b - c$. $\qquad$ If $a \le b$, then $a - c \le b - c$.

Notes:

Extra Practice

In Exercises 1–6, solve the inequality. Graph the solution.

1. $x - 3 < -4$

2. $-3 > -3 + h$

2.2 **Notetaking with Vocabulary** (continued)

3. $s - (-1) \geq 2$

4. $6 - 9 + u < -2$

5. $12 \leq 4c - 3c + 10$

6. $15 - 7p + 8p > 15 - 2$

7. You have $15 to spend on groceries. You have $12.25 worth of groceries already in your cart.

a. Write an inequality that represents how much more money m you can spend on groceries.

b. Solve the inequality.

2.3 Solving Inequalities Using Multiplication or Division
For use with Exploration 2.3

Essential Question How can you use division to solve an inequality?

1 EXPLORATION: Writing a Rule

Work with a partner.

a. Complete the table. Decide which graph represents the solution of the inequality $6 < 3x$. Write the solution of the inequality.

x	−1	0	1	2	3	4	5
3x	−3						
$6 \overset{?}{<} 3x$	No						

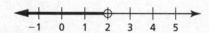 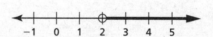

b. Use a table to solve each inequality. Then write a rule that describes how to use division to solve the inequalities.

i. $2x < 4$

ii. $3 \geq 3x$

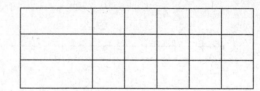

iii. $2x < 8$

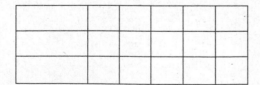

iv. $6 \geq 3x$

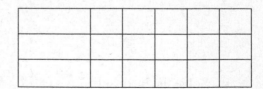

2.3 **Solving Inequalities Using Multiplication or Division** (continued)

2 **EXPLORATION: Writing a Rule**

Work with a partner.

a. Complete the table. Decide which graph represents the solution of the inequality
$6 < -3x$. Write the solution of the inequality.

x	−5	−4	−3	−2	−1	0	1
−3x							
$6 \overset{?}{<} -3x$							

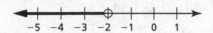 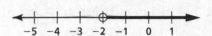

b. Use a table to solve each inequality. Then write a rule that describes how to use
division to solve the inequalities.

   i. $-2x < 4$ **ii.** $3 \geq -3x$

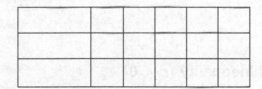 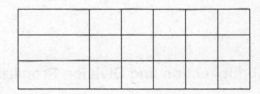

   iii. $-2x < 8$ **iv.** $6 \geq -3x$

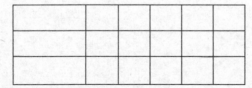 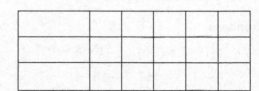

Communicate Your Answer

3. How can you use division to solve an inequality?

4. Use the rules you wrote in Explorations 1(b) and 2(b) to solve each inequality.

   a. $7x < -21$ **b.** $12 \leq 4x$ **c.** $10 < -5x$ **d.** $-3x \leq 0$

2.3 Notetaking with Vocabulary
For use after Lesson 2.3

Core Concepts

Multiplication and Division Properties of Inequality ($c > 0$)

Words Multiplying or dividing each side of an inequality by the same *positive* number produces an equivalent inequality.

Numbers

$-6 < 8$

$2 \cdot (-6) < 2 \cdot 8$

$-12 < 16$

$6 > -8$

$\dfrac{6}{2} > \dfrac{-8}{2}$

$3 > -4$

Algebra If $a > b$ and $c > 0$, then $ac > bc$.   If $a > b$ and $c > 0$, then $\dfrac{a}{c} > \dfrac{b}{c}$.

If $a < b$ and $c > 0$, then $ac < bc$.   If $a < b$ and $c > 0$, then $\dfrac{a}{c} < \dfrac{b}{c}$.

These properties are also true for $\leq$ and $\geq$.

Notes:

Multiplication and Division Properties of Inequality ($c < 0$)

Words When multiplying or dividing each side of an inequality by the same *negative* number, the direction of the inequality symbol must be reversed to produce an equivalent inequality.

Numbers

$-6 < 8$

$-2 \cdot (-6) > -2 \cdot 8$

$12 > -16$

$6 > -8$

$\dfrac{6}{-2} < \dfrac{-8}{-2}$

$-3 < 4$

Algebra If $a > b$ and $c < 0$, then $ac < bc$.   If $a > b$ and $c < 0$, then $\dfrac{a}{c} < \dfrac{b}{c}$.

If $a < b$ and $c < 0$, then $ac > bc$.   If $a < b$ and $c < 0$, then $\dfrac{a}{c} > \dfrac{b}{c}$.

These properties are also true for $\leq$ and $\geq$.

Notes:

2.3 Notetaking with Vocabulary (continued)

Extra Practice

In Exercises 1–8, solve the inequality. Graph the solution.

1. $6x < -30$

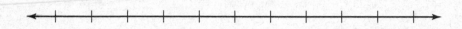

2. $48 \leq 16f$

3. $-\frac{6}{7} \leq \frac{3}{7}f$

4. $-4m \geq -16$

5. $\frac{x}{-6} > \frac{1}{3}$

2.3 **Notetaking with Vocabulary** (continued)

6. $1 \leq -\frac{1}{4}y$

7. $-\frac{2}{3} < -4x$

8. $-\frac{4}{5}x \geq -2$

9. There are at most 36 red and blue marbles in a bag. The number of red marbles is twice the number of blue marbles. Write and solve an inequality that represents the greatest number of red marbles r in the bag.

2.4 Solving Multi-Step Inequalities
For use with Exploration 2.4

Essential Question How can you solve a multi-step inequality?

1 EXPLORATION: Solving a Multi-Step Inequality

Go to *BigIdeasMath.com* for an interactive tool to investigate this exploration.

Work with a partner.

- Use what you already know about solving equations and inequalities to solve each multi-step inequality. Justify each step.

a. $2x + 3 \leq x + 5$

b. $-2x + 3 > x + 9$

c. $27 \geq 5x + 4x$

d. $-8x + 2x - 16 < -5x + 7x$

e. $3(x - 3) - 5x > -3x - 6$

f. $-5x - 6x \leq 8 - 8x - x$

2.4 **Solving Multi-Step Inequalities** (continued)

1 **EXPLORATION: Solving a Multi-Step Inequality** (continued)

- Match each inequality with its graph. Use a graphing calculator to check your answer.

a. $2x + 3 \leq x + 5$

b. $-2x + 3 > x + 9$

c. $27 \geq 5x + 4x$

d. $-8x + 2x - 16 < -5x + 7x$

e. $3(x - 3) - 5x > -3x - 6$

f. $-5x - 6x \leq 8 - 8x - x$

A.

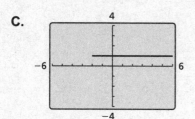

B.

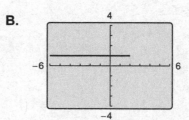

C.

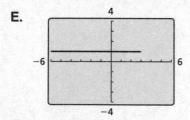

D.

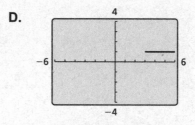

E.

F.

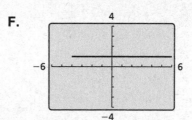

Communicate Your Answer

2. How can you solve a multi-step inequality?

3. Write two different multi-step inequalities whose solutions are represented by the graph.

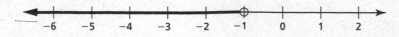

Name_____ Date_____

2.4 Notetaking with Vocabulary
For use after Lesson 2.4

Notes:

2.4 Notetaking with Vocabulary (continued)

Extra Practice

In Exercises 1–5, solve the inequality. Graph the solution.

1. $3x - 2 < 10$

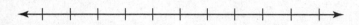

2. $4a + 8 \geq 0$

3. $2 + \dfrac{b}{-3} \leq 3$

4. $-\dfrac{c}{2} - 6 > -8$

5. $8 \leq -4(d + 1)$

2.4 **Notetaking with Vocabulary** (continued)

In Exercises 6–10, solve the inequality.

6. $5 - 2n > 8 - 4n$

7. $6h - 18 < 6h + 1$

8. $3p + 4 \geq -4p + 25$

9. $7j - 4j + 6 < -2 + 3j$

10. $12\left(\frac{1}{4}w + 3\right) \leq 3(w - 4)$

11. Find the value of k for which the solution of the inequality $k(4r - 5) \geq -12r - 9$ is all real numbers.

12. Find the value of k that makes the inequality $2kx - 3k < 2x + 4 + 3kx$ have no solution.

2.5 Solving Compound Inequalities
For use with Exploration 2.5

Essential Question How can you use inequalities to describe intervals on the real number line?

1) EXPLORATION: Describing Intervals on the Real Number Line

Work with a partner. In parts (a)–(d), use two inequalities to describe the interval.

a. Half-Open Interval

b. Half-Open Interval

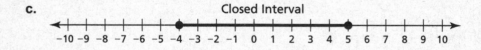

c. Closed Interval

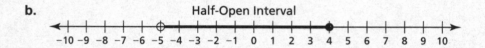

d. Open Interval

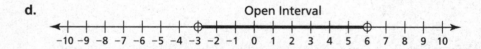

e. Do you use "and" or "or" to connect the two inequalities in parts (a)–(d)? Explain.

2.5 **Solving Compound Inequalities** (continued)

2 **EXPLORATION:** Describing Two Infinite Intervals

Work with a partner. In parts (a)–(d), use two inequalities to describe the interval.

a.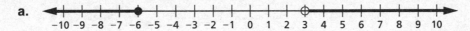

b.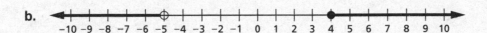

c.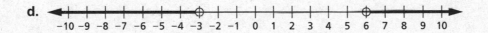

d.

e. Do you use "and" or "or" to connect the two inequalities in parts (a)–(d)?
   Explain.

Communicate Your Answer

3. How can you use inequalities to describe intervals on the real number line?

2.5 **Notetaking with Vocabulary**
For use after Lesson 2.5

In your own words, write the meaning of each vocabulary term.

compound inequality

Notes:

2.5 **Notetaking with Vocabulary** (continued)

Extra Practice

In Exercises 1–5, write the sentence as an inequality. Graph the inequality.

1. A number u is less than 7 and greater than 3.

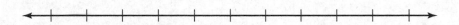

2. A number d is less than -2 or greater than or equal to 2.

3. A number s is no less than -2.4 and fewer than 4.2.

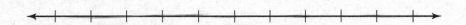

4. A number c is more than -4 or at most $-6\frac{1}{2}$.

5. A number c is no less than -1.5 and less than 5.3.

2.5   **Notetaking with Vocabulary** (continued)

In Exercises 6–10, solve the inequality. Graph the solution.

6. $4 < x - 3 \leq 7$

7. $15 \geq -5g \geq -10$

8. $z + 4 < 2 \ or \ -3z < -27$

9. $2t + 6 < 10 \ or \ -t + 7 \leq 2$

10. $-8 \leq \frac{1}{3}(6x + 24) \leq 12$

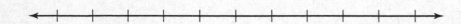

11. A certain machine operates properly when the relative humidity h satisfies the inequality $-60 \leq 2(h - 50) \leq 60$. Solve for h to find the range of values for which the machine operates properly.

2.6 Solving Absolute Value Inequalities
For use with Exploration 2.6

Essential Question How can you solve an absolute value inequality?

---

1 EXPLORATION: Solving an Absolute Value Inequality Algebraically

Work with a partner. Consider the absolute value inequality $|x + 2| \leq 3$.

a. Describe the values of $x + 2$ that make the inequality true. Use your description to write two linear inequalities that represent the solutions of the absolute value inequality.

b. Use the linear inequalities you wrote in part (a) to find the solutions of the absolute value inequality.

c. How can you use linear inequalities to solve an absolute value inequality?

---

2 EXPLORATION: Solving an Absolute Value Inequality Graphically

Go to *BigIdeasMath.com* **for an interactive tool to investigate this exploration.**

Work with a partner. Consider the absolute value inequality $|x + 2| \leq 3$.

a. On a real number line, locate the point for which $x + 2 = 0$.

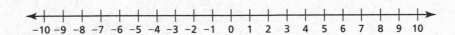

b. Locate the points that are within 3 units from the point you found in part (a). What do you notice about these points?

c. How can you use a number line to solve an absolute value inequality?

2.6 **Solving Absolute Value Inequalities** (continued)

---

3 **EXPLORATION:** Solving an Absolute Value Inequality Numerically

Go to *BigIdeasMath.com* for an interactive tool to investigate this exploration.

Work with a partner. Consider the absolute value inequality $|x + 2| \le 3$.

a. Use a spreadsheet, as shown, to solve the absolute value inequality.

	A	B
1	**x**	**|x + 2|**
2	-6	4
3	-5	
4	-4	
5	-3	
6	-2	
7	-1	
8	0	
9	1	
10	2	

abs(A2 + 2)

b. Compare the solutions you found using the spreadsheet with those you found in Explorations 1 and 2. What do you notice?

c. How can you use a spreadsheet to solve an absolute value inequality?

Communicate Your Answer

4. How can you solve an absolute value inequality?

5. What do you like or dislike about the algebraic, graphical, and numerical methods for solving an absolute value inequality? Give reasons for your answers.

2.6 Notetaking with Vocabulary
For use after Lesson 2.6

In your own words, write the meaning of each vocabulary term.

absolute value inequality

absolute deviation

Notes:

Core Concepts

Solving Absolute Value Inequalities

To solve $|ax + b| < c$ for $c > 0,$ solve the compound inequality

$$ax + b > -c \quad and \quad ax + b < c.$$

To solve $|ax + b| > c$ for $c > 0,$ solve the compound inequality

$$ax + b < -c \quad or \quad ax + b > c.$$

In the inequalities above, you can replace $<$ with $\leq$ and $>$ with $\geq$.

Notes:

2.6 **Notetaking with Vocabulary** (continued)

Extra Practice

In Exercises 1–9, solve the inequality. Graph the solution, if possible.

1. $|y + 2| < 8$

2. $\left|\dfrac{q}{3}\right| > 2$

3. $3|2a + 5| + 10 \le 37$

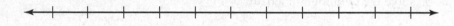

4. $|y - 3| \le 4$

5. $|3 + r| - 4 < 0$

2.6   **Notetaking with Vocabulary** (continued)

6. $|f + 12| > -4$

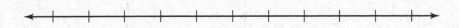

7. $\left|\dfrac{x}{4} - 7\right| < -2$

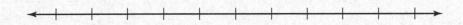

8. $|4x - 7| + 8 \geq 17$

9. $6|3 - k| + 14 > 14$

10. At a certain company, the average starting salary s for a new worker is $25,000. The actual salary has an absolute deviation of at most $1800. Write and solve an inequality to find the range of the starting salaries.

Name _____ Date _____

Plot the point in a coordinate plane. Describe the location of the point.

1. $A(-3, 1)$ **2.** $B(2, 2)$ **3.** $C(1, 0)$ **4.** $D(5, 2)$

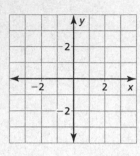 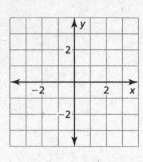 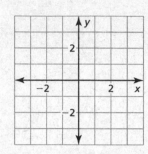 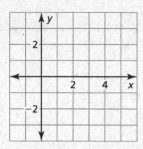

5. Plot the point that is on the y-axis and 5 units down from the origin.

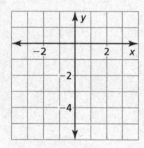

Evaluate the expression for the given value of x.

6. $2x + 1$; $x = 3$ **7.** $16 - 4x$; $x = -4$ **8.** $12x + 7$; $x = -2$ **9.** $-9 - 3x$; $x = 5$

10. The length of a side of a square is represented by $(24 - 3x)$ feet. What is the length of the side of the square when $x = 6$?

3.1 Functions
For use with Exploration 3.1

Essential Question What is a function?

---

1 EXPLORATION: Describing a Function

Work with a partner. Functions can be described in many ways.

- by an equation
- by an input-output table
- using words
- by a graph
- as a set of ordered pairs

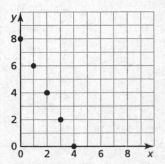

a. Explain why the graph shown represents a function.

b. Describe the function in two other ways.

---

2 EXPLORATION: Identifying Functions

Work with a partner. Determine whether each relation represents a function. Explain your reasoning.

a.

Input, x	0	1	2	3	4
Output, y	8	8	8	8	8

b.

Input, x	8	8	8	8	8
Output, y	0	1	2	3	4

3.1 **Functions** (continued)

2 **EXPLORATION: Identifying Functions** (continued)

c. **Input, x** **Output, y**

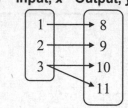

d.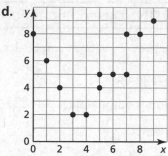

e. $(-2, 5), (-1, 8), (0, 6), (1, 6), (2, 7)$ f. $(-2, 0), (-1, 0), (-1, 1), (0, 1), (1, 2), (2, 2)$

g. Each radio frequency x in a listening area has exactly one radio station y.

h. The same television station x can be found on more than one channel y.

i. $x = 2$

j. $y = 2x + 3$

Communicate Your Answer

3. What is a function? Give examples of relations, other than those in Explorations 1 and 2, that (a) are functions and (b) are not functions.

Name_____ Date_____

3.1 Notetaking with Vocabulary
For use after Lesson 3.1

In your own words, write the meaning of each vocabulary term.

relation

function

domain

range

independent variable

dependent variable

Notes:

3.1 Notetaking with Vocabulary (continued)

Core Concepts

Vertical Line Test

Words A graph represent a function when no vertical line passes through more than one point on the graph.

Examples Function   Not a function

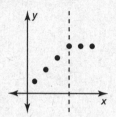   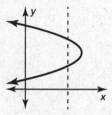

Notes:

The Domain and Range of a Function

The **domain** of a function is the set of all possible input values.

The **range** of a function is the set of all possible output values.

Notes:

3.1 **Notetaking with Vocabulary** (continued)

Extra Practice

In Exercises 1 and 2, determine whether the relation is a function. Explain.

1.

Input, x	–2	0	1	–2
Output, y	4	5	4	5

2. $(0, 3), (1, 1), (2, 1), (3, 0)$

In Exercises 3 and 4, determine whether the graph represents a function. Explain.

3.
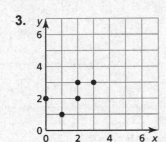

4.
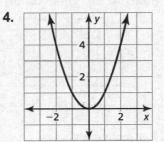

In Exercises 5 and 6, find the domain and range of the function represented by the graph.

5.
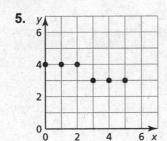

6.
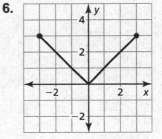

7. The function $y = 12x$ represents the number y of pages of text a computer printer can print in x minutes.

   a. Identify the independent and dependent variables.

   b. The domain is 1, 2, 3, and 4. What is the range?

3.2 Linear Functions
For use with Exploration 3.2

Essential Question How can you determine whether a function is linear or nonlinear?

---

1 **EXPLORATION:** Finding Patterns for Similar Figures

Go to *BigIdeasMath.com* **for an interactive tool to investigate this exploration.**

Work with a partner. Complete each table for the sequence of similar figures. (In parts (a) and (b), use the rectangle shown.) Graph the data in each table. Decide whether each pattern is linear or nonlinear. Justify your conclusion.

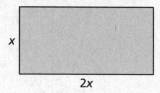

x

2x

a. perimeters of similar rectangles

x	1	2	3	4	5
P					

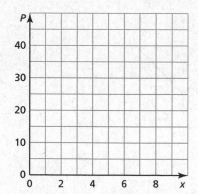

b. areas of similar rectangles

x	1	2	3	4	5
A					

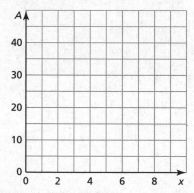

3.2 **Linear Functions** (continued)

1 **EXPLORATION: Finding Patterns for Similar Figures** (continued)

c. circumferences of circles of radius *r*

r	1	2	3	4	5
C					

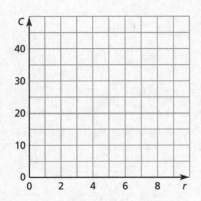

d. areas of circles of radius *r*

r	1	2	3	4	5
A					

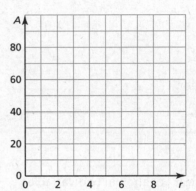

Communicate Your Answer

2. How do you know that the patterns you found in Exploration 1 represent functions?

3. How can you determine whether a function is linear or nonlinear?

4. Describe two real-life patterns: one that is linear and one that is nonlinear. Use patterns that are different from those described in Exploration 1.

3.2 Notetaking with Vocabulary
For use after Lesson 3.2

In your own words, write the meaning of each vocabulary term.

linear equation in two variables

linear function

nonlinear function

solution of a linear equation in two variables

discrete domain

continuous domain

Notes:

Name_____ Date_____

Core Concepts

Representations of Functions

Words An output is 3 more than the input.

Equation $y = x + 3$

| **Input-Output Table** | | **Mapping Diagram** | **Graph** |

Input-Output Table

Input, x	Output, y
−1	2
0	3
1	4
2	5

Mapping Diagram

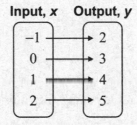

Graph

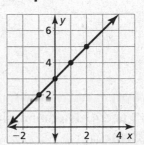

Notes:

Discrete and Continuous Domains

A **discrete domain** is a set of input values that consists of only certain numbers in an interval.

Example: Integers from 1 to 5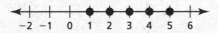

A **continuous domain** is a set of input values that consists of all numbers in an interval.

Example: All numbers from 1 to 5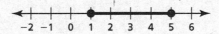

Notes:

3.2 **Notetaking with Vocabulary** (continued)

Extra Practice

In Exercises 1 and 2, determine whether the graph represents a *linear* or *nonlinear* function. Explain.

1.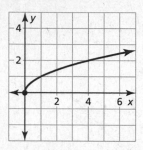

2.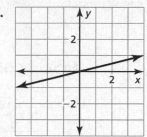

In Exercises 3 and 4, determine whether the table represents a *linear* or *nonlinear* function. Explain.

3.

x	1	2	3	4
y	−1	2	5	8

4.

x	−1	0	1	2
y	0	−1	0	3

In Exercises 5 and 6, determine whether the equation represents a *linear* or *nonlinear* function. Explain.

5. $y = 3 - 2x$

6. $y = -\dfrac{3}{4}x^3$

In Exercises 7 and 8, find the domain of the function represented by the graph. Determine whether the domain is *discrete* or *continuous*. Explain.

7.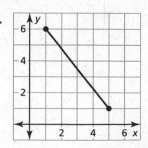

8.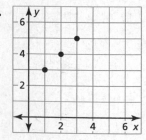

Name_____ Date_____

3.3 Function Notation
For use with Exploration 3.3

Essential Question How can you use function notation to represent a function?

1 **EXPLORATION: Matching Functions with Their Graphs**

Work with a partner. Match each function with its graph.

a. $f(x) = 2x - 3$

b. $g(x) = -x + 2$

c. $h(x) = x^2 - 1$

d. $j(x) = 2x^2 - 3$

A.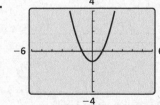

B.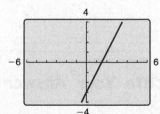

C.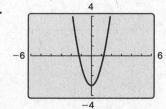

D.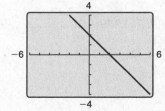

3.3 **Function Notation** (continued)

---

2 **EXPLORATION:** Evaluating a Function

Go to *BigIdeasMath.com* for an interactive tool to investigate this exploration.

Work with a partner. Consider the function

$$f(x) = -x + 3.$$

Locate the points $(x, f(x))$ on the graph.

Explain how you found each point.

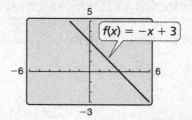

a. $(-1, f(-1))$

b. $(0, f(0))$

c. $(1, f(1))$

d. $(2, f(2))$

Communicate Your Answer

3. How can you use function notation to represent a function? How are standard notation and function notation similar? How are they different?

Standard Notation	*Function Notation*
$y = 2x + 5$	$f(x) = 2x + 5$

3.3 Notetaking with Vocabulary
For use after Lesson 3.3

In your own words, write the meaning of each vocabulary term.

function notation

Notes:

3.3 Notetaking with Vocabulary (continued)

Extra Practice

In Exercises 1–6, evaluate the function when $x = -4$, 0, and 2.

1. $f(x) = -x + 4$

2. $g(x) = 5x$

3. $h(x) = 7 - 2x$

4. $s(x) = 12 - 0.25x$

5. $t(x) = 6 + 3x - 2$

6. $u(x) = -2 - 2x + 7$

7. Let $n(t)$ be the number of DVDs you have in your collection after t trips to the video store. Explain the meaning of each statement.

    a. $n(0) = 8$

    b. $n(3) = 14$

    c. $n(5) > n(3)$

    d. $n(7) - n(2) = 10$

In Exercises 8–11, find the value of x so that the function has the given value.

8. $b(x) = -3x + 1;\ b(x) = -20$

9. $r(x) = 4x - 3;\ r(x) = 33$

10. $m(x) = -\frac{3}{5}x - 4;\ m(x) = 2$

11. $w(x) = \frac{5}{6}x - 3;\ w(x) = -18$

3.3 **Notetaking with Vocabulary** (continued)

In Exercises 12 and 13, graph the linear function.

12. $s(x) = \frac{1}{2}x - 2$

x	−4	−2	0	2	4
s(x)					

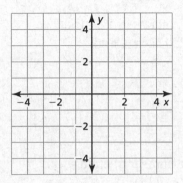

13. $t(x) = 1 - 2x$

x	−2	−1	0	1	2
t(x)					

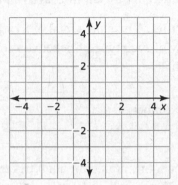

14. The function $B(m) = 50m + 150$ represents the balance (in dollars) in your savings account after m months. The table shows the balance in your friend's savings account. Who has the better savings plan? Explain.

Month	Balance
2	$330
4	$410
6	$490

3.4 Graphing Linear Equations in Standard Form
For use with Exploration 3.4

Essential Question How can you describe the graph of the equation $Ax + By = C$?

---

1 **EXPLORATION:** Using a Table to Plot Points

Go to *BigIdeasMath.com* for an interactive tool to investigate this exploration.

Work with a partner. You sold a total of $16 worth of tickets to a fundraiser. You lost track of how many of each type of ticket you sold. Adult tickets are $4 each. Child tickets are $2 each.

$$\boxed{} \atop \text{adult} \quad \bullet \quad \begin{array}{c}\text{Number of}\\ \text{adult tickets}\end{array} \quad + \quad {\boxed{} \atop \text{child}} \quad \bullet \quad \begin{array}{c}\text{Number of}\\ \text{child tickets}\end{array} \quad = \quad \boxed{}$$

a. Let x represent the number of adult tickets. Let y represent the number of child tickets. Use the verbal model to write an equation that relates x and y.

b. Complete the table to show the different combinations of tickets you might have sold.

x				
y				

c. Plot the points from the table. Describe the pattern formed by the points.

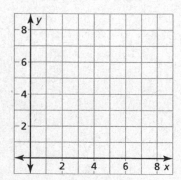

d. If you remember how many adult tickets you sold, can you determine how many child tickets you sold? Explain your reasoning.

3.4 **Graphing Linear Equations in Standard Form** (continued)

2 **EXPLORATION:** Rewriting and Graphing an Equation

Go to *BigIdeasMath.com* for an interactive tool to investigate this exploration.

Work with a partner. You sold a total of $48 worth of cheese. You forgot how many pounds of each type of cheese you sold. Swiss cheese costs $8 per pound. Cheddar cheese costs $6 per pound.

$$\frac{\boxed{}}{\text{pound}} \cdot \begin{array}{c}\text{Pounds of}\\ \text{Swiss}\end{array} + \frac{\boxed{}}{\text{pound}} \cdot \begin{array}{c}\text{Pounds of}\\ \text{cheddar}\end{array} = \boxed{}$$

a. Let x represent the number of pounds of Swiss cheese. Let y represent the number of pounds of cheddar cheese. Use the verbal model to write an equation that relates x and y.

b. Solve the equation for y. Then use a graphing calculator to graph the equation. Given the real-life context of the problem, find the domain and range of the function.

c. The *x*-intercept of a graph is the *x*-coordinate of a point where the graph crosses the *x*-axis. The *y*-intercept of a graph is the *y*-coordinate of a point where the graph crosses the *y*-axis. Use the graph to determine the *x*- and *y*-intercepts.

d. How could you use the equation you found in part (a) to determine the *x*- and *y*-intercepts? Explain your reasoning.

e. Explain the meaning of the intercepts in the context of the problem.

Communicate Your Answer

3. How can you describe the graph of the equation $Ax + By = C$?

4. Write a real-life problem that is similar to those shown in Explorations 1 and 2.

3.4 Notetaking with Vocabulary
For use after Lesson 3.4

In your own words, write the meaning of each vocabulary term.

standard form

x-intercept

y-intercept

Core Concepts

Horizontal and Vertical Lines

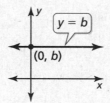

The graph of $y = b$ is a horizontal line.
The line passes through the point $(0, b)$.

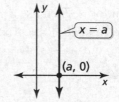

The graph of $x = a$ is a vertical line.
The line passes through the point $(a, 0)$.

Notes:

3.4 Notetaking with Vocabulary (continued)

Using Intercepts to Graph Equations

The **x-intercept** of a graph is the x-coordinate of a point where the graph crosses the x-axis. It occurs when $y = 0$.

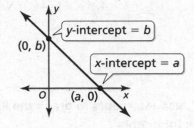

The **y-intercept** of a graph is the y-coordinate of a point where the graph crosses the y-axis. It occurs when $x = 0$.

To graph the linear equation $Ax + By = C$, find the intercepts and draw the line that passes through the two intercepts.

- To find the x-intercept, let $y = 0$ and solve for x.

- To find the y-intercept, let $x = 0$ and solve for y.

Notes:

Extra Practice

In Exercises 1 and 2, graph the linear equation.

1. $y = -3$

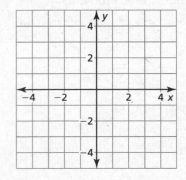

2. $x = 2$

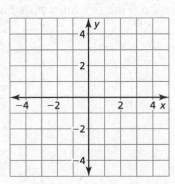

Name _____ Date _____

In Exercises 3–5, find the *x*- and *y*-intercepts of the graph of the linear equation.

3. $3x + 4y = 12$

4. $-x - 4y = 16$

5. $5x - 2y = -30$

In Exercises 6 and 7, use intercepts to graph the linear equation. Label the points corresponding to the intercepts.

6. $-8x + 12y = 24$

7. $2x + y = 4$

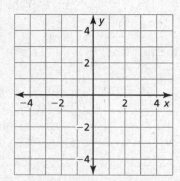
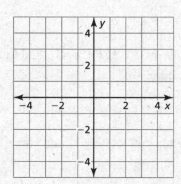

8. The school band is selling sweatshirts and baseball caps to raise $9000 to attend a band competition. Sweatshirts cost $25 each and baseball caps cost $10 each. The equation $25x + 10y = 9000$ models this situation, where *x* is the number of sweatshirts sold and *y* is the number of baseball caps sold.

   a. Find and interpret the intercepts.

   b. If 258 sweatshirts are sold, how many baseball caps are sold?

   c. Graph the equation. Find two more possible solutions in the context of the problem.

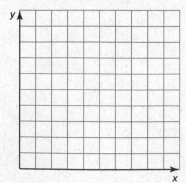

3.5 Graphing Linear Equations in Slope-Intercept Form
For use with Exploration 3.5

Essential Question How can you describe the graph of the equation $y = mx + b$?

1 EXPLORATION: Finding Slopes and y-Intercepts

Work with a partner. Find the slope and y-intercept of each line.

a.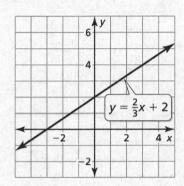

$y = \frac{2}{3}x + 2$

b.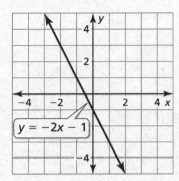

$y = -2x - 1$

2 EXPLORATION: Writing a Conjecture

Go to *BigIdeasMath.com* for an interactive tool to investigate this exploration.

Work with a partner. Graph each equation. Then complete the table. Use the completed table to write a conjecture about the relationship between the graph of $y = mx + b$ and the values of m and b.

Equation	Description of graph	Slope of graph	y-Intercept
a. $y = -\frac{2}{3}x + 3$	Line	$-\frac{2}{3}$	3
b. $y = 2x - 2$			
c. $y = -x + 1$			
d. $y = x - 4$			

a.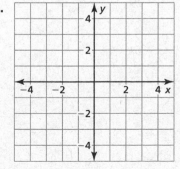

b.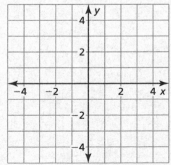

3.5 **Graphing Linear Equation in Slope-Intercept Form** (continued)

2 **EXPLORATION:** Writing a Conjecture (continued)

c.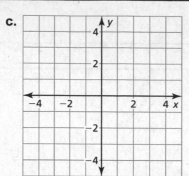

d.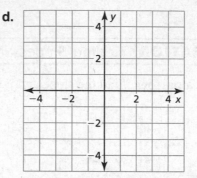

Communicate Your Answer

3. How can you describe the graph of the equation $y = mx + b$?

    a. How does the value of m affect the graph of the equation?

    b. How does the value of b affect the graph of the equation?

    c. Check your answers to parts (a) and (b) by choosing one equation from Exploration 2 and (1) varying only m and (2) varying only b.

3.5 Notetaking with Vocabulary
For use after Lesson 3.5

In your own words, write the meaning of each vocabulary term.

slope

rise

run

slope-intercept form

constant function

Core Concepts

Slope

The **slope** m of a nonvertical line passing through two points (x_1, y_1) and (x_2, y_2) is the ratio of the **rise** (change in y) to the **run** (change in x).

$$\text{slope} = m = \frac{\text{rise}}{\text{run}} = \frac{\text{change in } y}{\text{change in } x} = \frac{y_2 - y_1}{x_2 - x_1}$$

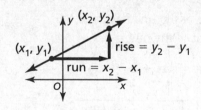

When the line rises from left to right, the slope is positive. When the line falls from left to right, the slope is negative.

Notes:

3.5 **Notetaking with Vocabulary** (continued)

Slope

Positive slope	*Negative slope*	*Slope of 0*	*Undefined slope*
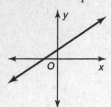	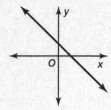	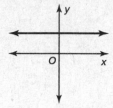	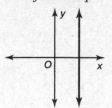
The line rises from left to right.	The line falls from left to right.	The line is horizontal.	The line is vertical.

Notes:

Slope-Intercept Form

Words A linear equation written in the form
$y = mx + b$ is in **slope-intercept form**.
The slope of the line is m, and the
y-intercept of the line is b.

Algebra $y = mx + b$

slope y-intercept

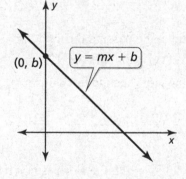

Notes:

Name_____ Date_____

3.5 Notetaking with Vocabulary (continued)

Extra Practice

In Exercise 1–3, describe the slope of the line. Then find the slope.

1.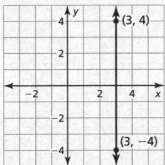

2.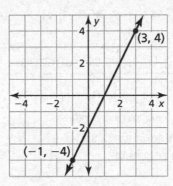

3.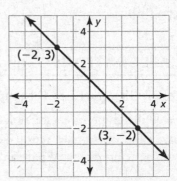

In Exercise 4 and 5, the points represented by the table lie on a line. Find the slope of the line.

4.

x	1	2	3	4
y	−2	−2	−2	−2

5.

x	−3	−1	1	3
y	11	3	−5	−13

In Exercise 6–8, find the slope and the y-intercept of the graph of the linear equation.

6. $6x + 4y = 24$

7. $y = -\frac{3}{4}x + 2$

8. $y = 5x$

9. A linear function f models a relationship in which the dependent variable decreases 6 units for every 3 units the independent variable decreases. The value of the function at 0 is 4. Graph the function. Identify the slope, y-intercept, and x-intercept of the graph.

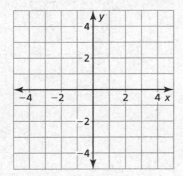

3.6 Transformations of Graphs of Linear Functions
For use with Exploration 3.6

Essential Question How does the graph of the linear function $f(x) = x$ compare to the graphs of $g(x) = f(x) + c$ and $h(x) = f(cx)$?

---

1 EXPLORATION: Comparing Graphs of Functions

Work with a partner. The graph of $f(x) = x$ is shown.

Sketch the graph of each function, along with f, on the same set of coordinate axes. Use a graphing calculator to check your results. What can you conclude?

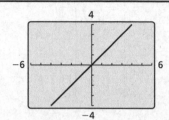

a. $g(x) = x + 4$ **b.** $g(x) = x + 2$ **c.** $g(x) = x - 2$ **d.** $g(x) = x - 4$

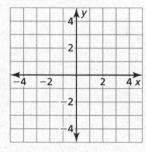 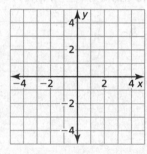 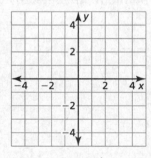 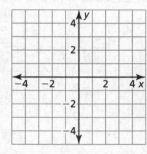

---

2 EXPLORATION: Comparing Graphs of Functions

Work with a partner. Sketch the graph of each function, along with $f(x) = x$, on the same set of coordinate axes. Use a graphing calculator to check your results. What can you conclude?

a. $h(x) = \frac{1}{2}x$ **b.** $h(x) = 2x$ **c.** $h(x) = -\frac{1}{2}x$ **d.** $h(x) = -2x$

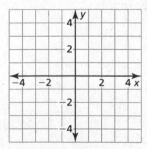 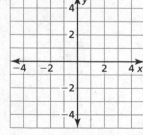 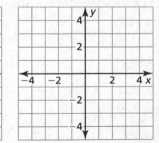 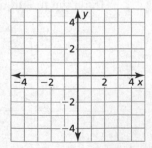

3.6 **Transformations of Graphs of Linear Functions (continued)**

---

3 **EXPLORATION: Matching Functions with Their Graphs**

Work with a partner. Match each function with its graph. Use a graphing calculator to check your results. Then use the results of Explorations 1 and 2 to compare the graph of k to the graph of $f(x) = x$.

a. $k(x) = 2x - 4$

b. $k(x) = -2x + 2$

c. $k(x) = \frac{1}{2}x + 4$

d. $k(x) = -\frac{1}{2}x - 2$

A.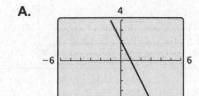

B.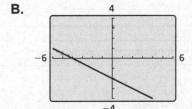

C.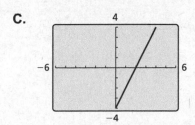

D.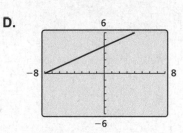

Communicate Your Answer

4. How does the graph of the linear function $f(x) = x$ compare to the graphs of $g(x) = f(x) + c$ and $h(x) = f(cx)$?

Name ____ Date __________

3.6 Notetaking with Vocabulary
For use after Lesson 3.6

In your own words, write the meaning of each vocabulary term.

family of functions

parent function

transformation

translation

reflection

horizontal shrink

horizontal stretch

vertical stretch

vertical shrink

Notes:

Name_____ Date_____

3.6 **Notetaking with Vocabulary** (continued)

Core Concepts

A **translation** is a transformation that shifts a graph horizontally or vertically but does not change the size, shape, or orientation of the graph.

Horizontal Translations

The graph of $y = f(x - h)$ is a horizontal translation of the graph of $y = f(x)$, where $h \neq 0$.

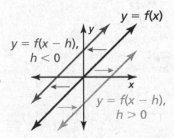

Subtracting h from the *inputs* before evaluating the function shifts the graph left when $h < 0$ and right when $h > 0$.

Vertical Translations

The graph of $y = f(x) + k$ is a vertical translation of the graph of $y = f(x)$, where $k \neq 0$.

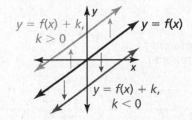

Adding k to the *outputs* shifts the graph down when $k < 0$ and up when $k > 0$.

Notes:

A **reflection** is a transformation that flips a graph over a line called the *line of reflection*.

Reflections in the *x*-axis

The graph of $y = -f(x)$ is a reflection in the *x*-axis of the graph of $y = f(x)$.

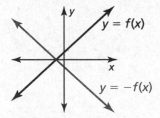

Multiplying the outputs by -1 changes their signs.

Reflections in the *y*-axis

The graph of $y = f(-x)$ is a reflection in the *y*-axis of the graph of $y = f(x)$.

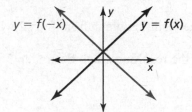

Multiplying the inputs by -1 changes their signs.

Notes:

3.6 Notetaking with Vocabulary (continued)

Horizontal Stretches and Shrinks

The graph of $y = f(ax)$ is a horizontal stretch or shrink by a factor of $\dfrac{1}{a}$ of the graph of $y = f(x)$, where $a > 0$ and $a \neq 1$.

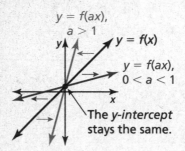

Vertical Stretches and Shrinks

The graph of $y = a \bullet f(x)$ is a vertical stretch or shrink by a factor of a of the graph of $y = f(x)$, where $a > 0$ and $a \neq 1$.

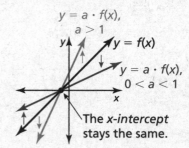

Notes:

Transformations of Graphs

The graph of $y = a \bullet f(x - h) + k$ or the graph of $y = f(ax - h) + k$ can be obtained from the graph of $y = f(x)$ by performing these steps.

Step 1   Translate the graph of $y = f(x)$ horizontally h units.

Step 2   Use a to stretch or shrink the resulting graph from Step 1.

Step 3   Reflect the resulting graph from Step 2 when $a < 0$.

Step 4   Translate the resulting graph from Step 3 vertically k units.

Notes:

3.6 Notetaking with Vocabulary (continued)

Extra Practice

In Exercises 1–6, use the graphs of *f* and *g* to describe the transformation from the graph of *f* to the graph of *g*.

1.
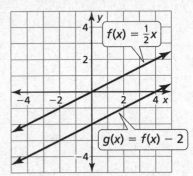

$f(x) = \frac{1}{2}x$

$g(x) = f(x) - 2$

2.
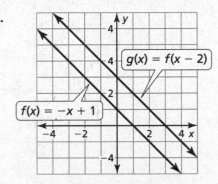

$g(x) = f(x - 2)$

$f(x) = -x + 1$

3.
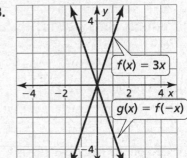

$f(x) = 3x$

$g(x) = f(-x)$

4.
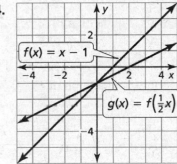

$f(x) = x - 1$

$g(x) = f\left(\frac{1}{2}x\right)$

5.
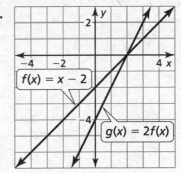

$f(x) = x - 2$

$g(x) = 2f(x)$

6.
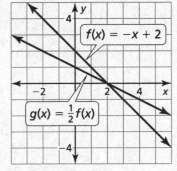

$f(x) = -x + 2$

$g(x) = \frac{1}{2}f(x)$

7. Graph $f(x) = x$ and $g(x) = 3x - 2$.
   Describe the transformations from the graph of *f* to the graph of *g*.

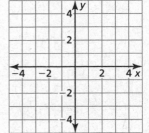

Chapter 4 **Maintaining Mathematical Proficiency**

Use the graph to answer the question.

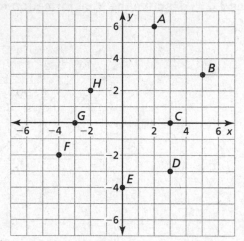

1. What ordered pair corresponds to point *A*?   2. What ordered pair corresponds to point *H*?

3. What ordered pair corresponds to point *E*?   4. Which point is located in Quadrant III?

5. Which point is located in Quadrant IV?   6. Which point is located on the negative *x*-axis?

Solve the equation for *y*.

7. $x - y = -12$ 8. $8x + 4y = 16$ 9. $3x - 5y + 15 = 0$

10. $0 = 3y - 6x + 12$ 11. $y - 2 = 3x + 4y$ 12. $6y + 3 - 2x = x$

13. Rectangle *ABCD* has vertices $A(4, -2)$, $B(4, 5)$, and $C(7, 5)$. What are the coordinates of vertex *D*?

4.1 Writing Equations in Slope-Intercept Form
For use with Exploration 4.1

Essential Question Given the graph of a linear function, how can you write an equation of the line?

1 EXPLORATION: Writing Equations in Slope-Intercept Form

Go to _BigIdeasMath.com_ for an interactive tool to investigate this exploration.

Work with a partner.

- Find the slope and *y*-intercept of each line.
- Write an equation of each line in slope-intercept form.
- Use a graphing calculator to verify your equation.

a.
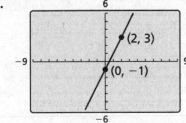

b.
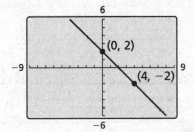

c.
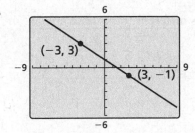

d.
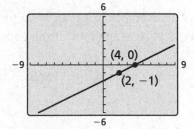

4.1 **Writing Equations in Slope-Intercept Form** (continued)

2 **EXPLORATION:** Mathematical Modeling

Work with a partner. The graph shows the cost of a smartphone plan.

a. What is the *y*-intercept of the line? Interpret the *y*-intercept in the context of the problem.

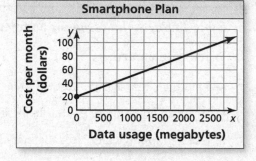

b. Approximate the slope of the line. Interpret the slope in the context of the problem.

c. Write an equation that represents the cost as a function of data usage.

Communicate Your Answer

3. Given the graph of a linear function, how can you write an equation of the line?

4. Give an example of a graph of a linear function that is different from those above. Then use the graph to write an equation of the line.

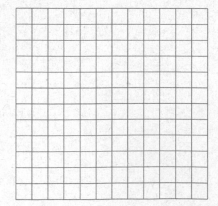

Name_____ Date_____

Notetaking with Vocabulary
For use after Lesson 4.1

In your own words, write the meaning of each vocabulary term.

linear model

Notes:

4.1 Notetaking with Vocabulary (continued)

Extra Practice

In Exercises 1–6, write an equation of the line with the given slope and *y*-intercept.

1. slope: 0
    y-intercept: 9

2. slope: −1
    y-intercept: 0

3. slope: 2
    y-intercept: −3

4. slope: −3
    y-intercept: 7

5. slope: 4
    y-intercept: −2

6. slope: $\frac{1}{3}$
    y-intercept: 2

In Exercises 7–12, write an equation of the line in slope-intercept form.

7.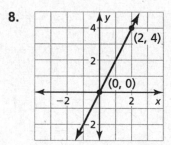

8.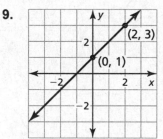

9.

10.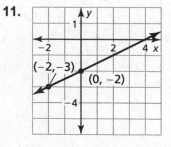

11.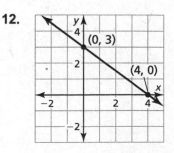

12.

Name_____ Date_____

In Exercises 13–18, write an equation of the line that passes through the given points.

13. $(0, -4), (8, 4)$ **14.** $(2, 1), (0, -7)$ **15.** $(0, 2), (4, 3)$

16. $(0, -5), (-4, -1)$ **17.** $(8, 0), (0, 8)$ **18.** $(0, 3), (2, -5)$

In Exercises 19–24, write a linear function f with the given values.

19. $f(0) = -5, f(4) = -3$ **20.** $f(-5) = 5, f(0) = 10$ **21.** $f(0) = 5, f(9) = -4$

22. $f(0) = 10, f(7) = -4$ **23.** $f(-2) = -2, f(0) = 2$ **24.** $f(0) = 16, f(2) = 8$

25. An electrician charges an initial fee of \$50 and \$190 after 4 hours of work.

   a. Write a linear model that represents the total cost as a function of the number of hours worked.

   b. How much does the electrician charge per hour?

4.2 Writing Equations in Point-Slope Form
For use with Exploration 4.2

Essential Question How can you write an equation of a line when you are given the slope and a point on the line?

1 EXPLORATION: Writing Equations of Lines

Go to *BigIdeasMath.com* for an interactive tool to investigate this exploration.

Work with a partner.

- Sketch the line that has the given slope and passes through the given point.
- Find the *y*-intercept of the line.
- Write an equation of the line.

a. $m = \dfrac{1}{2}$

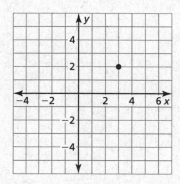

b. $m = -2$

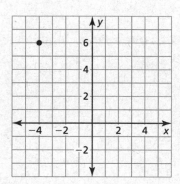

2 EXPLORATION: Writing a Formula

Work with a partner.

The point (x_1, y_1) is a given point on a nonvertical line. The point (x, y) is any other point on the line. Write an equation that represents the slope m of the line. Then rewrite this equation by multiplying each side by the difference of the *x*-coordinates to obtain the **point-slope form** of a linear equation.

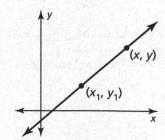

4.2 **Writing Equations in Point-Slope Form** (continued)

---

3 **EXPLORATION:** Writing an Equation

Go to *BigIdeasMath.com* for an interactive tool to investigate this exploration.

Work with a partner.

For four months, you have saved $25 per month.
You now have $175 in your savings account.

a. Use your result from Exploration 2 to
   write an equation that represents the
   balance A after t months.

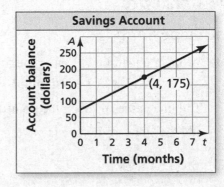

b. Use a graphing calculator to verify your equation.

Communicate Your Answer

4. How can you write an equation of a line when you are given the slope and a point
   on the line?

5. Give an example of how to write an equation of a line when you are given the
   slope and a point on the line. Your example should be different from those above.

Name_____ Date _____

In your own words, write the meaning of each vocabulary term.

point-slope form

Core Concepts

Point-Slope Form

Words A linear equation written in the form

$y - y_1 = m(x - x_1)$ is in **point-slope form**.

The line passes through the point (x_1, y_1),

and the slope of the line is m.

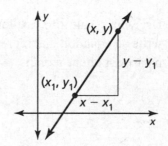

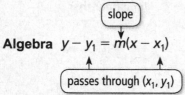

Algebra $y - y_1 = m(x - x_1)$

Notes:

Name_____ Date_____

Extra Practice

In Exercises 1–6, write an equation in point-slope form of the line that passes through the given point and has the given slope.

1. $(-2, 1); m = -3$

2. $(3, 5); m = 2$

3. $(-1, -2); m = -1$

4. $(5, 0); m = \dfrac{4}{3}$

5. $(0, 4); m = 7$

6. $(1, 2); m = -\dfrac{1}{2}$

In Exercises 7–12, write an equation in slope-intercept form of the line shown.

7.
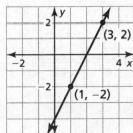

8.
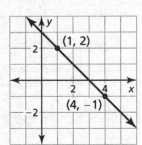

9.
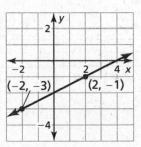

10.
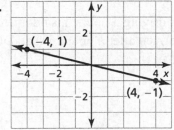

11.
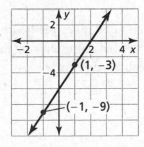

12.
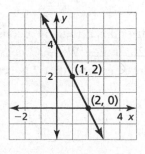

4.2 **Notetaking with Vocabulary** (continued)

In Exercises 13–18, write a linear function *f* with the given values.

13. $f(-3) = -1, f(-2) = 4$ 14. $f(-2) = 1, f(1) = 7$ 15. $f(-1) = 2, f(3) = 3$

16. $f(0) = -2, f(4) = -1$ 17. $f(1) = 0, f(0) = 8$ 18. $f(3) = 5, f(2) = 6$

In Exercises 19 and 20, tell whether the data in the table can be modeled by a linear equation. Explain. If possible, write a linear equation that represents *y* as a function of *x*.

19.

x	–3	–1	0	1	3
y	–110	–60	–35	–10	40

20.

x	–3	–1	0	1	3
y	–98	18	8	62	142

21. Your friend is driving at a constant speed of 60 miles per hour. After driving 3 hours, his odometer reads 265 miles. Write a linear function *D* that represents the miles driven after *h* hours. What does the odometer read after 7 hours of continuous driving?

4.3 **Writing Equations of Parallel and Perpendicular Lines**
For use with Exploration 4.3

Essential Question How can you recognize lines that are parallel or perpendicular?

1 **EXPLORATION: Recognizing Parallel Lines**

Go to *BigIdeasMath.com* **for an interactive tool to investigate this exploration.**

Work with a partner. Write each linear equation in slope-intercept form. Then use a graphing calculator to graph the three equations in the same square viewing window. (The graph of the first equation is shown.) Which two lines appear parallel? How can you tell?

a. $3x + 4y = 6$

$3x + 4y = 12$

$4x + 3y = 12$

b. $5x + 2y = 6$

$2x + y = 3$

$2.5x + y = 5$

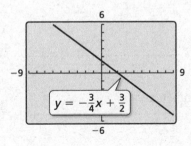

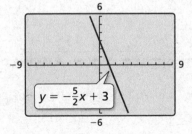

4.3 **Writing Equations of Parallel and Perpendicular Lines** (continued)

2 **EXPLORATION:** Recognizing Perpendicular Lines

Go to *BigIdeasMath.com* for an interactive tool to investigate this exploration.

Work with a partner. Write each linear equation in slope-intercept form. Then use a graphing calculator to graph the three equations in the same square viewing window. (The graph of the first equation is shown.) Which two lines appear perpendicular? How can you tell?

a. $3x + 4y = 6$

$3x - 4y = 12$

$4x - 3y = 12$

b. $2x + 5y = 10$

$-2x + y = 3$

$2.5x - y = 5$

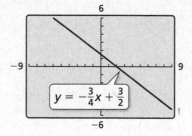

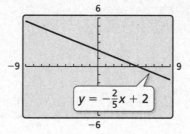

Communicate Your Answer

3. How can you recognize lines that are parallel or perpendicular?

4. Compare the slopes of the lines in Exploration 1. How can you use slope to determine whether two lines are parallel? Explain your reasoning.

5. Compare the slopes of the lines in Exploration 2. How can you use slope to determine whether two lines are perpendicular? Explain your reasoning.

4.3 Notetaking with Vocabulary
For use after Lesson 4.3

In your own words, write the meaning of each vocabulary term.

parallel lines

perpendicular lines

Core Concepts

Parallel Lines and Slopes

Two lines in the same plane that never intersect are **parallel lines**. Two distinct nonvertical lines are parallel if and only if they have the same slope.

All vertical lines are parallel.

Notes:

Perpendicular Lines and Slopes

Two lines in the same plane that intersect to form right angles are **perpendicular lines**. Nonvertical lines are perpendicular if and only if their slopes are negative reciprocals.

Vertical lines are perpendicular to horizontal lines.

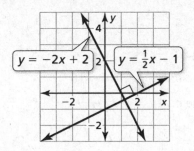

Notes:

4.3 Notetaking with Vocabulary (continued)

Extra Practice

In Exercises 1–6, determine which of the lines, if any, are parallel. Explain.

1.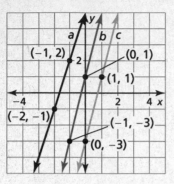

2.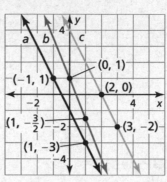

3. Line a passes through $(-4, -1)$ and $(2, 2)$.

   Line b passes through $(-5, -3)$ and $(5, 1)$.

   Line c passes through $(-2, -3)$ and $(2, -1)$.

4. Line a passes through $(-2, 5)$ and $(2, 1)$.

   Line b passes through $(-4, 3)$ and $(3, 4)$.

   Line c passes through $(-3, 4)$ and $(2, -6)$.

5. Line a: $4x = -3y + 9$

   Line b: $8y = -6x + 16$

   Line c: $4y = -3x + 9$

6. Line a: $5y - x = 4$

   Line b: $5y = x + 7$

   Line c: $5y - 2x = 5$

In Exercises 7 and 8, write an equation of the line that passes through the given point and is parallel to the given line.

7. $(3, -1)$; $y = \frac{1}{3}x - 3$

8. $(1, -2)$; $y = -2x + 1$

4.3 Notetaking with Vocabulary (continued)

In Exercises 9–14, determine which of the lines, if any, are parallel or perpendicular. Explain.

9.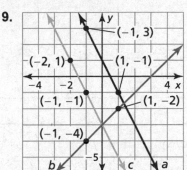

10.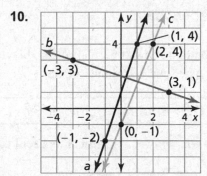

11. Line a passes through $(-2, 4)$ and $(1, 1)$.

Line b passes through $(2, 1)$ and $(4, 4)$.

Line c passes through $(1, -2)$ and $(-1, 4)$.

12. Line a passes through $(-2, -4)$ and $(-1, -1)$.

Line b passes through $(-1, -4)$ and $(1, 2)$.

Line c passes through $(2, 3)$ and $(4, 2)$.

13. Line a: $y = \frac{3}{4}x + 1$

Line b: $-3y = 4x - 3$

Line c: $4y = -3x + 9$

14. Line a: $5y - 2x = 1$

Line b: $y = \frac{5}{2}x - 1$

Line c: $y = \frac{2}{5}x + 3$

In Exercises 15 and 16, write an equation of the line that passes through the given point and is perpendicular to the given line.

15. $(-2, 2)$; $y = \frac{2}{3}x + 2$

16. $(3, 1)$; $2y = 4x - 3$

4.4 Scatter Plots and Lines of Fit
For use with Exploration 4.4

Essential Question How can you use a scatter plot and a line of fit to make conclusions about data?

A **scatter plot** is a graph that shows the relationship between two data sets. The two data sets are graphed as ordered pairs in a coordinate plane.

1 EXPLORATION: Finding a Line of Fit

Go to *BigIdeasMath.com* for an interactive tool to investigate this exploration.

Work with a partner. A survey was taken of 179 married couples. Each person was asked his or her age. The scatter plot shows the results.

a. Draw a line that approximates the data. Write an equation of the line. Explain the method you used.

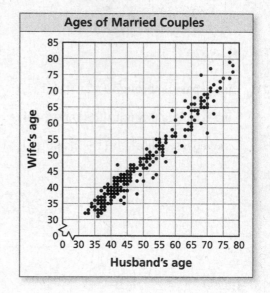

b. What conclusions can you make from the equation you wrote? Explain your reasoning.

4.4 **Scatter Plots and Lines of Fit** (continued)

2 **EXPLORATION:** Finding a Line of Fit

Go to *BigIdeasMath.com* **for an interactive tool to investigate this exploration.**

Work with a partner. The scatter plot shows the median ages of American women at their first marriage for selected years from 1960 through 2010.

Ages of American Women at First Marriage

a. Draw a line that approximates the data. Write an equation of the line. Let *x* represent the number of years since 1960. Explain the method you used.

b. What conclusions can you make from the equation you wrote?

c. Use your equation to predict the median age of American women at their first marriage in the year 2020.

Communicate Your Answer

3. How can you use a scatter plot and a line of fit to make conclusions about data?

4. Use the Internet or some other reference to find a scatter plot of real-life data that is different from those given above. Then draw a line that approximates the data and write an equation of the line. Explain the method you used.

4.4 # Notetaking with Vocabulary
For use after Lesson 4.4

In your own words, write the meaning of each vocabulary term.

scatter plot

correlation

line of fit

Core Concepts

Scatter Plot

A **scatter plot** is a graph that shows the relationship between two data sets. The two data sets are graphed as ordered pairs in a coordinate plane. Scatter plots can show trends in the data.

Notes:

4.4 **Notetaking with Vocabulary** (continued)

Using a Line of Fit to Model Data

Step 1 Make a scatter plot of the data.

Step 2 Decide whether the data can be modeled by a line.

Step 3 Draw a line that appears to fit the data closely. There should be approximately as many points above the line as below it.

Step 4 Write an equation using two points on the line. The points do not have to represent actual data pairs, but they must lie on the line of fit.

Notes:

Extra Practice

1. The scatter plot shows the weights (in pounds) of a baby over time.

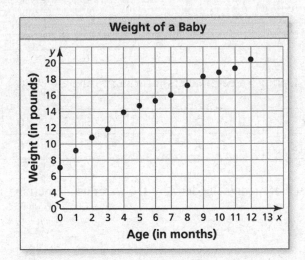

a. What is the weight of the baby when the baby is four months old?

b. What is the age of the baby when the baby weighs 17.2 pounds?

c. What tends to happen to weight of the baby as the age increases?

4.4 **Notetaking with Vocabulary** (continued)

In Exercises 2–5, tell whether x and y show a *positive*, a *negative*, or *no* correlation.

2.

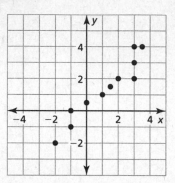

3.

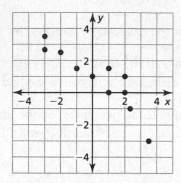

4.

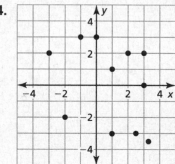

5.

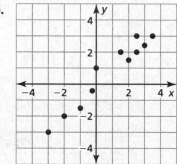

6. The table shows the depth y (in centimeters) of water filling a bathtub after x minutes.

Time (minutes), x	0	2	4	6	8	10	12
Depth (centimeters), y	6	8	11	14	17	20	24

a. Write an equation that models the depth of the water as a function of time.

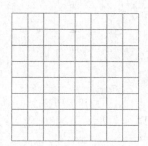

b. Interpret the slope and y-intercept of the line of fit.

4.5 Analyzing Lines of Fit
For use with Exploration 4.5

Essential Question How can you *analytically* find a line of best fit for a scatter plot?

---

1 EXPLORATION: Finding a Line of Best Fit

Go to *BigIdeasMath.com* for an interactive tool to investigate this exploration.

Work with a partner.
The scatter plot shows the median ages of American women at their first marriage for selected years from 1960 through 2010. In Exploration 2 in Section 4.4, you approximated a line of fit graphically. To find the line of *best* fit, you can use a computer, spreadsheet, or graphing calculator that has a *linear regression* feature.

a. The data from the scatter plot is shown in the table. Note that 0, 5, 10, and so on represent the numbers of years since 1960. What does the ordered pair (25, 23.3) represent?

b. Use the *linear regression* feature to find an equation of the line of best fit. You should obtain results such as those shown below.

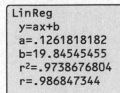

c. Write an equation of the line of best fit. Compare your result with the equation you obtained in Exploration 2 in Section 4.4.

4.5 **Analyzing Lines of Fit** (continued)

Communicate Your Answer

2. How can you *analytically* find a line of best fit for a scatter plot?

3. The data set relates the number of chirps per second for striped ground crickets and the outside temperature in degrees Fahrenheit. Make a scatter plot of the data. Then find an equation of the line of best fit. Use your result to estimate the outside temperature when there are 19 chirps per second.

Chirps per second	20.0	16.0	19.8	18.4	17.1
Temperature (°F)	88.6	71.6	93.3	84.3	80.6

Chirps per second	14.7	15.4	16.2	15.0	14.4
Temperature (°F)	69.7	69.4	83.3	79.6	76.3

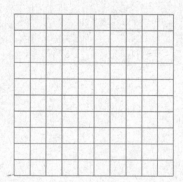

Name_____ Date_____

4.5 Notetaking with Vocabulary
For use after Lesson 4.5

In your own words, write the meaning of each vocabulary term.

residual

linear regression

line of best fit

correlation coefficient

interpolation

extrapolation

causation

Notes:

4.5 Notetaking with Vocabulary (continued)

Core Concepts

Residuals

A **residual** is the difference of
the y-value of a data point and the
corresponding y-value found using
the line of fit. A residual can be
positive, negative, or zero.

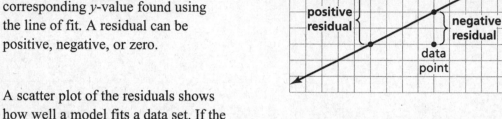

A scatter plot of the residuals shows
how well a model fits a data set. If the
model is a good fit, then the absolute
values of the residuals are relatively
small, and the residual points will be more or less evenly dispersed about the horizontal
axis. If the model is not a good fit, then the residual points will form some type of
pattern that suggests the data are not linear. Wildly scattered residual points suggest that
the data might have no correlation.

Notes:

Extra Practice

**In Exercises 1 and 2, use residuals to determine whether the model is a good fit
for the data in the table. Explain.**

1. $y = -3x + 2$

x	−4	−3	−2	−1	0	1	2	3	4
y	13	11	8	6	3	0	−4	−8	−10

4.5 **Notetaking with Vocabulary** (continued)

2. $y = -0.5x + 1$

x	0	1	2	3	4	5	6	7	8
y	2	0	-3	-5	-7	-6	-4	-3	-1

3. The table shows the numbers *y* of visitors to a particular beach and the average daily temperatures *x*.

   a. Use a graphing calculator to find an equation of the line of best fit. Then plot the data and graph the equation in the same viewing window.

Average Daily Temperature (°F)	Number of Beach Visitors
80	100
82	150
83	145
85	190
86	215
88	263
89	300
90	350

   b. Identify and interpret the correlation coefficient.

   c. Interpret the slope and *y*-intercept of the line of best fit.

4.6 Arithmetic Sequences
For use with Exploration 4.6

Essential Question How can you use an arithmetic sequence to describe a pattern?

An **arithmetic sequence** is an ordered list of numbers in which the difference between each pair of consecutive **terms**, or numbers in the list, is the same.

---

1 **EXPLORATION:** Describing a Pattern

Go to *BigIdeasMath.com* for an interactive tool to investigate this exploration.

Work with a partner. Use the figures to complete the table. Plot the points given by your completed table. Describe the pattern of the *y*-values.

a. $n = 1$ $n = 2$ $n = 3$ $n = 4$ $n = 5$

Number of stars, *n*	1	2	3	4	5
Number of sides, *y*					

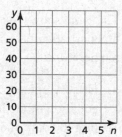

b. $n = 1$ $n = 2$ $n = 3$ $n = 4$ $n = 5$

n	1	2	3	4	5
Number of circles, *y*					

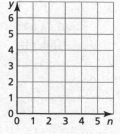

4.6 **Arithmetic Sequences** (continued)

1 **EXPLORATION: Describing a Pattern** (continued)

c. $n = 1$ $n = 2$ $n = 3$ $n = 4$ $n = 5$

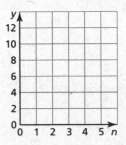

Number of rows, n	1	2	3	4	5
Number of dots, y					

Communicate Your Answer

2. How can you use an arithmetic sequence to describe a pattern? Give an example from real life.

3. In chemistry, water is called H_2O because each molecule of water has two hydrogen atoms and one oxygen atom. Describe the pattern shown below. Use the pattern to determine the number of atoms in 23 molecules.

$n = 1$ $n = 2$ $n = 3$ $n = 4$ $n = 5$

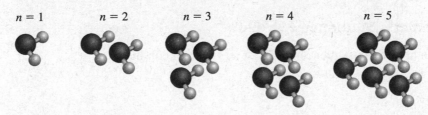

4.6 Notetaking with Vocabulary
For use after Lesson 4.6

In your own words, write the meaning of each vocabulary term.

sequence

term

arithmetic sequence

common difference

Core Concepts

Arithmetic Sequence

In an **arithmetic sequence**, the difference between each pair of consecutive terms is the same. This difference is called the **common difference**. Each term is found by adding the common difference to the previous term.

$5, \quad 10, \quad 15, \quad 20, \ldots$ Terms of an arithmetic sequence

$+5 \quad +5 \quad +5 \longleftarrow$ [common difference]

Notes:

Equation for an Arithmetic Sequence

Let a_n be the nth term of an arithmetic sequence with first term a_1 and common difference d. The nth term is given by

$$a_n = a_1 + (n - 1)d.$$

Notes:

Name_____ Date_____

Extra Practice

In Exercises 1–6, write the next three terms of the arithmetic sequence.

1. 1, 8, 15, 22, …

2. 20, 14, 8, 2, …

3. 12, 21, 30, 39, …

4. 5, 12, 19, 26, …

5. 3, 7, 11, 15, …

6. 2, 14, 26, 38, …

In Exercises 7–12, graph the arithmetic sequence.

7. 1, 3, 5, 7, …

8. 9, 6, 3, 0, …

9. $\frac{15}{2}, \frac{13}{2}, \frac{11}{2}, \frac{9}{2}, \ldots$

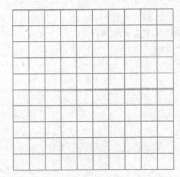 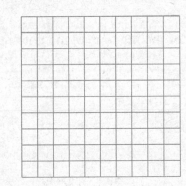 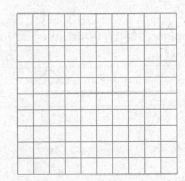

10. 1, 2.5, 4, 5.5, …

11. 1, 4, 7, 10, …

12. $\frac{1}{4}, \frac{5}{4}, \frac{9}{4}, \frac{13}{4}, \ldots$

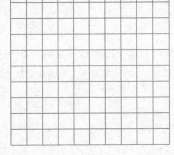  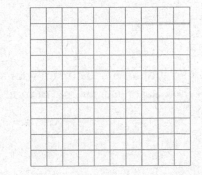

4.6 **Notetaking with Vocabulary** (continued)

In Exercises 13–15, determine whether the graph represents an arithmetic sequence. Explain.

13.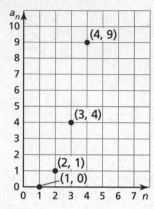

14.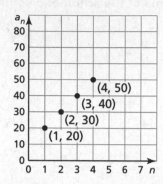

15.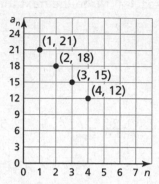

In Exercises 16–21, write an equation for the nth term of the arithmetic sequence. Then find a_{10}.

16. $-5.4, -6.6, -7.8, -9.0, \ldots$

17. $43, 38, 33, 28, \ldots$

18. $6, 10, 14, 18, \ldots$

19. $-11, -9, -7, -5, \ldots$

20. $34, 37, 40, 43, \ldots$

21. $\dfrac{9}{4}, \dfrac{7}{4}, \dfrac{5}{4}, \dfrac{3}{4}, \ldots$

22. In an auditorium, the first row of seats has 30 seats. Each row behind the first row has 4 more seats than the row in front of it. How many seats are in the 25th row?

Chapter 5 Maintaining Mathematical Proficiency

Graph the equation.

1. $y + 2 = x$

2. $2x - y = 3$

3. $5x + 2y = 10$

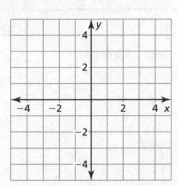 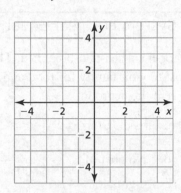 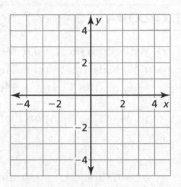

4. $y - 3 = x$

5. $3x - y = -2$

6. $3x + 4y = 12$

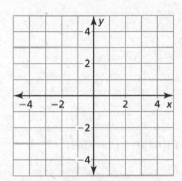 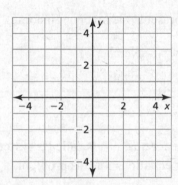 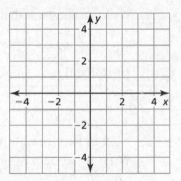

Solve the inequality. Graph the solution.

7. $a - 3 > -2$

8. $-4 \geq -2c$

 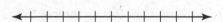

9. $2d - 5 < -3$

10. $8 - 3r \leq 5 - 2r$

5.1 Solving Systems of Linear Equations by Graphing
For use with Exploration 5.1

Essential Question How can you solve a system of linear equations?

1 EXPLORATION: Writing a System of Linear Equations

Work with a partner. Your family opens a bed-and-breakfast. They spend $600 preparing a bedroom to rent. The cost to your family for food and utilities is $15 per night. They charge $75 per night to rent the bedroom.

a. Write an equation that represents the costs.

$$\begin{array}{c}\text{Cost, } C \\ \text{(in dollars)}\end{array} = \begin{array}{c}\$15 \text{ per} \\ \text{night}\end{array} \cdot \begin{array}{c}\text{Number of} \\ \text{nights, } x\end{array} + \$600$$

b. Write an equation that represents the revenue (income).

$$\begin{array}{c}\text{Revenue, } R \\ \text{(in dollars)}\end{array} = \begin{array}{c}\$75 \text{ per} \\ \text{night}\end{array} \cdot \begin{array}{c}\text{Number of} \\ \text{nights, } x\end{array}$$

c. A set of two (or more) linear equations is called a **system of linear equations.** Write the system of linear equations for this problem.

2 EXPLORATION: Using a Table or Graph to Solve a System

Go to *BigIdeasMath.com* for an interactive tool to investigate this exploration.

Work with a partner. Use the cost and revenue equations from Exploration 1 to determine how many nights your family needs to rent the bedroom before recovering the cost of preparing the bedroom. This is the *break-even point*.

a. Complete the table.

x (nights)	0	1	2	3	4	5	6	7	8	9	10	11
C (dollars)												
R (dollars)												

5.1 **Solving Systems of Linear Equations by Graphing** (continued)

2 **EXPLORATION: Using a Table or Graph to Solve a System** (continued)

   b. How many nights does your family need to rent the bedroom before breaking even?

   c. In the same coordinate plane, graph the cost equation and the revenue equation from Exploration 1.

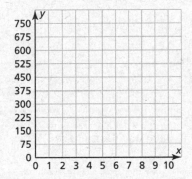

   d. Find the point of intersection of the two graphs. What does this point represent? How does this compare to the break-even point in part (b)? Explain.

Communicate Your Answer

   3. How can you solve a system of linear equations? How can you check your solution?

   4. Solve each system by using a table or sketching a graph. Explain why you chose each method. Use a graphing calculator to check each solution.

   a. $y = -4.3x - 1.3$ **b.** $y = x$ **c.** $y = -x - 1$

       $y = 1.7x + 4.7$ $y = -3x + 8$ $y = 3x + 5$

5.1 Notetaking with Vocabulary
For use after Lesson 5.1

In your own words, write the meaning of each vocabulary term.

system of linear equations

solution of a system of linear equations

Core Concepts

Solving a System of Linear Equations by Graphing

Step 1 Graph each equation in the same coordinate plane.

Step 2 Estimate the point of intersection.

Step 3 Check the point from Step 2 by substituting for x and y in each equation of the original system.

Notes:

5.1 **Notetaking with Vocabulary** (continued)

Extra Practice

In Exercises 1–6, tell whether the ordered pair is a solution of the system of linear equations.

1. $(3, 1);$ $x + y = 4$
$2x - y = 3$

2. $(1, 3);$ $x - y = -2$
$2x + y = 5$

3. $(2, 0);$ $y = x - 2$
$y = -3x + 6$

4. $(-1, -2);$ $x - 2y = 3$
$2x - y = 0$

5. $(-2, 3);$ $3x - 2y = -12$
$2x + 4y = 9$

6. $(4, -3);$ $2x + 2y = 2$
$3x - 3y = 21$

In Exercises 7–9, use the graph to solve the system of linear equations. Check your solution.

7. $3x - 2y = 10$
$x + y = 0$

8. $x - 2y = 5$
$2x + y = -5$

9. $x + 2y = 8$
$3x - 2y = 8$

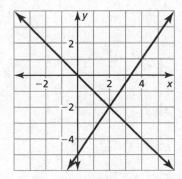 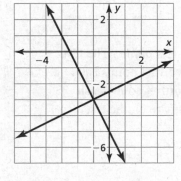 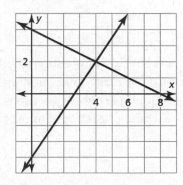

5.1 **Notetaking with Vocabulary** (continued)

In Exercises 10–15, solve the system of linear equations by graphing.

10. $y = -x + 3$
$y = x + 5$

11. $y = \frac{1}{2}x + 2$
$y = -\frac{1}{2}x + 4$

12. $3x - 2y = 6$
$y = -3$

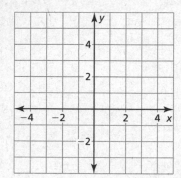
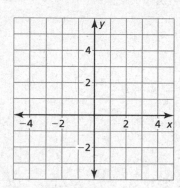
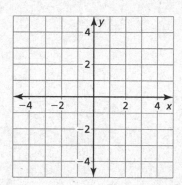

13. $y = 4x$
$y = -4x + 8$

14. $y = \frac{1}{4}x + 3$
$y = \frac{3}{4}x + 5$

15. $3x - 4y = 7$
$5x + 2y = 3$

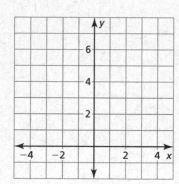
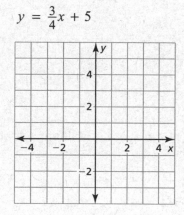
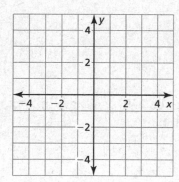

16. A test has twenty questions worth 100 points. The test consists of x true-false questions worth 4 points each and y multiple choice questions worth 8 points each. How many of each type of question are on the test?

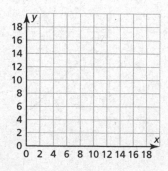

5.2 Solving Systems of Linear Equations by Substitution
For use with Exploration 5.2

Essential Question How can you use substitution to solve a system of linear equations?

---

1 EXPLORATION: Using Substitution to Solve Systems

Work with a partner. Solve each system of linear equations using two methods.

Method 1   Solve for x first.

Solve for x in one of the equations. Substitute the expression for x into the other equation to find y. Then substitute the value of y into one of the original equations to find x.

Method 2   Solve for y first.

Solve for y in one of the equations. Substitute the expression for y into the other equation to find x. Then substitute the value of x into one of the original equations to find y.

Is the solution the same using both methods? Explain which method you would prefer to use for each system.

a. $x + y = -7$
$-5x + y = 5$

b. $x - 6y = -11$
$3x + 2y = 7$

c. $4x + y = -1$
$3x - 5y = -18$

5.2 Solving Systems of Linear Equations by Substitution (continued)

2 EXPLORATION: Writing and Solving a System of Equations

Go to *BigIdeasMath.com* for an interactive tool to investigate this exploration.

Work with a partner.

a. Write a random ordered pair with integer coordinates. One way to do this is to use a graphing calculator. The ordered pair generated at the right is $(-2, -3)$.

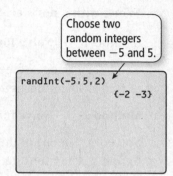

Choose two random integers between -5 and 5.

```
randInt(-5,5,2)
              {-2 -3}
```

b. Write a system of linear equations that has your ordered pair as its solution.

c. Exchange systems with your partner and use one of the methods from Exploration 1 to solve the system. Explain your choice of method.

Communicate Your Answer

3. How can you use substitution to solve a system of linear equations?

4. Use one of the methods from Exploration 1 to solve each system of linear equations. Explain your choice of method. Check your solutions.

a. $x + 2y = -7$
   $2x - y = -9$

b. $x - 2y = -6$
   $2x + y = -2$

c. $-3x + 2y = -10$
   $-2x + y = -6$

d. $3x + 2y = 13$
   $x - 3y = -3$

e. $3x - 2y = 9$
   $-x - 3y = 8$

f. $3x - y = -6$
   $4x + 5y = 11$

5.2 Notetaking with Vocabulary
For use after Lesson 5.2

In your own words, write the meaning of each vocabulary term.

system of linear equations

solution of a system of linear equations

Core Concepts

Solving a System of Linear Equations by Substitution

Step 1 Solve one of the equations for one of the variables.

Step 2 Substitute the expression from Step 1 into the other equation and solve for the other variable.

Step 3 Substitute the value from Step 2 into one of the original equations and solve.

Notes:

5.2   Notetaking with Vocabulary (continued)

Extra Practice

In Exercises 1–18, solve the system of linear equations by substitution. Check your solution.

1. $2x + 2y = 10$
$y = 5 + x$

2. $2x - y = 3$
$x = -2y - 1$

3. $x - 3y = -1$
$x = y$

4. $x - 2y = -3$
$y = x + 1$

5. $2x + y = 3$
$x = 3y + 5$

6. $3x + y = -5$
$y = 2x + 5$

7. $y = 2x + 8$
$y = -2x$

8. $y = \frac{3}{4}x + 1$
$y = \frac{1}{4}x + 3$

9. $2x - 3y = 0$
$y = 4$

Name_____ Date_____

10. $x + y = 3$

$2x + 4y = 8$

11. $y = \frac{1}{2}x + 1$

$y = -\frac{1}{2}x + 9$

12. $3x - 2y = 3$

$4x - y = 4$

13. $7x - 4y = 8$

$5x - y = 2$

14. $y = \frac{3}{5}x - 12$

$y = \frac{1}{3}x - 8$

15. $3x - 4y = -1$

$5x + 2y = 7$

16. $y = -x + 3$

$x + 2y = 0$

17. $y - 5x = -2$

$-4x + y = 2$

18. $4x - 8y = 3$

$8x + 4y = 1$

19. An adult ticket to a museum costs $3 more than a children's ticket. When 200 adult tickets and 100 children's tickets are sold, the total revenue is $2100. What is the cost of a children's ticket?

5.3 Solving Systems of Linear Equations by Elimination
For use with Exploration 5.3

Essential Question How can you use elimination to solve a system of linear equations?

---

1 EXPLORATION: Writing and Solving a System of Equations

Work with a partner. You purchase a drink and a sandwich for $4.50. Your friend purchases a drink and five sandwiches for $16.50. You want to determine the price of a drink and the price of a sandwich.

a. Let x represent the price (in dollars) of one drink. Let y represent the price (in dollars) of one sandwich. Write a system of equations for the situation. Use the following verbal model.

$$\begin{array}{ccccc} \text{Number} \\ \text{of drinks} \end{array} \bullet \begin{array}{c} \text{Price} \\ \text{per drink} \end{array} + \begin{array}{c} \text{Number of} \\ \text{sandwiches} \end{array} \bullet \begin{array}{c} \text{Price per} \\ \text{sandwich} \end{array} = \begin{array}{c} \text{Total} \\ \text{price} \end{array}$$

Label one of the equations Equation 1 and the other equation Equation 2.

b. Subtract Equation 1 from Equation 2. Explain how you can use the result to solve the system of equations. Then find and interpret the solution.

---

2 EXPLORATION: Using Elimination to Solve Systems

Work with a partner. Solve each system of linear equations using two methods.

Method 1 **Subtract.** Subtract Equation 2 from Equation 1.Then use the result to solve the system.

Method 2 **Add.** Add the two equations. Then use the result to solve the system.

Is the solution the same using both methods? Which method do you prefer?

a. $3x - y = 6$
$3x + y = 0$

b. $2x + y = 6$
$2x - y = 2$

c. $x - 2y = -7$
$x + 2y = 5$

5.3 **Solving Systems of Linear Equations by Elimination** (continued)

3 **EXPLORATION:** Using Elimination to Solve a System

Work with a partner.

$$2x + y = 7 \qquad \text{Equation 1}$$
$$x + 5y = 17 \qquad \text{Equation 2}$$

a. Can you eliminate a variable by adding or subtracting the equations as they are? If not, what do you need to do to one or both equations so that you can?

b. Solve the system individually. Then exchange solutions with your partner and compare and check the solutions.

Communicate Your Answer

4. How can you use elimination to solve a system of linear equations?

5. When can you add or subtract the equations in a system to solve the system? When do you have to multiply first? Justify your answers with examples.

6. In Exploration 3, why can you multiply an equation in the system by a constant and not change the solution of the system? Explain your reasoning.

5.3 Notetaking with Vocabulary
For use after Lesson 5.3

In your own words, write the meaning of each vocabulary term.

coefficient

Core Concepts

Solving a System of Linear Equations by Elimination

Step 1 Multiply, if necessary, one or both equations by a constant so at least one pair of like terms has the same or opposite coefficients.

Step 2 Add or subtract the equations to eliminate one of the variables.

Step 3 Solve the resulting equation.

Step 4 Substitute the value from Step 3 into one of the original equations and solve for the other variable.

Notes:

5.3 **Notetaking with Vocabulary** (continued)

Extra Practice

In Exercises 1–18, solve the system of linear equations by elimination. Check your solution.

1. $x + 3y = 17$

$-x + 2y = 8$

2. $2x - y = 5$

$5x + y = 16$

3. $2x + 3y = 10$

$-2x - y = -2$

4. $4x + 3y = 6$

$-x - 3y = 3$

5. $5x + 2y = -28$

$-5x + 3y = 8$

6. $2x - 5y = 8$

$3x + 5y = -13$

7. $2x + y = 12$

$3x - 18 = y$

8. $4x + 3y = 14$

$2y = 6 + 4x$

9. $-4x = -2 + 4y$

$-4y = 1 - 4x$

5.3 **Notetaking with Vocabulary** (continued)

10. $x + 2y = 20$
$2x + y = 19$

11. $3x - 2y = -2$
$4x - 3y = -4$

12. $9x + 4y = 11$
$3x - 10y = -2$

13. $4x + 3y = 21$
$5x + 2y = 21$

14. $-3x - 5y = -7$
$-4x - 3y = -2$

15. $8x + 4y = 12$
$7x + 3y = 10$

16. $4x + 3y = -7$
$-2x - 5y = 7$

17. $8x - 3y = -9$
$5x + 4y = 12$

18. $-3x + 5y = -2$
$2x - 2y = 1$

19. The sum of two numbers is 22. The difference is 6. What are the two numbers?

5.4 Solving Special Systems of Linear Equations
For use with Exploration 5.4

Essential Question   Can a system of linear equations have no solution or infinitely many solutions?

1 EXPLORATION: Using a Table to Solve a System

Go to *BigIdeasMath.com* for an interactive tool to investigate this exploration.

Work with a partner. You invest $450 for equipment to make skateboards. The materials for each skateboard cost $20. You sell each skateboard for $20.

   a. Write the cost and revenue equations. Then complete the table for your cost C and your revenue R.

x (skateboards)	0	1	2	3	4	5	6	7	8	9	10
C (dollars)											
R (dollars)											

   b. When will your company break even? What is wrong?

2 EXPLORATION: Writing and Analyzing a System

Go to *BigIdeasMath.com* for an interactive tool to investigate this exploration.

Work with a partner. A necklace and matching bracelet have two types of beads. The necklace has 40 small beads and 6 large beads and weighs 10 grams. The bracelet has 20 small beads and 3 large beads and weighs 5 grams. The threads holding the beads have no significant weight.

   a. Write a system of linear equations that represents the situation. Let x be the weight (in grams) of a small bead and let y be the weight (in grams) of a large bead.

   b. Graph the system in the coordinate plane shown. What do you notice about the two lines?

   c. Can you find the weight of each type of bead? Explain your reasoning.

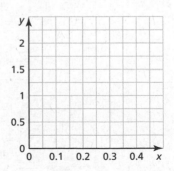

5.4 **Solving Special Systems of Linear Equations** (continued)

Communicate Your Answer

3. Can a system of linear equations have no solution or infinitely many solutions? Give examples to support your answers.

4. Does the system of linear equations represented by each graph have *no solution, one solution,* or *infinitely many solutions*? Explain.

a.

$y = x + 2$

$x + y = 2$

b.

$y = x + 2$

$-x + y = 1$

c.

$y = x + 2$

$-2x + 2y = 4$

5.4 Notetaking with Vocabulary
For use after Lesson 5.4

In your own words, write the meaning of each vocabulary term.

parallel

Core Concepts

Solutions of Systems of Linear Equations

A system of linear equations can have *one solution*, *no solution*, or *infinitely many solutions*.

One solution	No solution	Infinitely many solutions
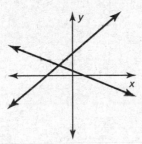	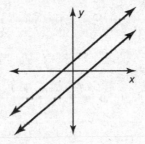	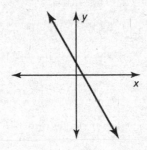
The lines intersect.	The lines are parallel.	The lines are the same.

Notes:

5.4   Notetaking with Vocabulary (continued)

Extra Practice

In Exercises 1–18, solve the system of linear equations.

1. $y = 3x - 7$
   $y = 3x + 4$

2. $y = 5x - 1$
   $y = -5x + 5$

3. $2x - 3y = 10$
   $-2x + 3y = -10$

4. $x + 3y = 6$
   $-x - 3y = 3$

5. $6x + 6y = -3$
   $-6x - 6y = 3$

6. $2x - 5y = -3$
   $3x + 5y = 8$

7. $2x + 3y = 1$
   $-2x + 3y = -7$

8. $4x + 3y = 17$
   $-8x - 6y = 34$

9. $3x - 2y = 6$
   $-9x + 6y = -18$

5.4 **Notetaking with Vocabulary** (continued)

10. $-2x + 5y = -21$
$2x - 5y = 21$

11. $3x - 8y = 3$
$8x - 3y = 8$

12. $18x + 12y = 24$
$3x + 2y = 6$

13. $15x - 6y = 9$
$5x - 2y = 27$

14. $-3x - 5y = 8$
$6x + 10y = -16$

15. $2x - 4y = 2$
$-2x - 4y = 6$

16. $5x + 7y = 7$
$7x + 5y = 5$

17. $y = \frac{2}{3}x + 7$
$y = \frac{2}{3}x - 5$

18. $-3x + 5y = 15$
$9x - 15y = -45$

19. You have \$15 in savings. Your friend has \$25 in savings. You both start saving \$5 per week. Write a system of linear equations that represents this situation. Will you ever have the same amount of savings as your friend? Explain.

5.5 Solving Equations by Graphing
For use with Exploration 5.5

Essential Question   How can you use a system of linear equations to solve an equation with variables on both sides?

---

1   EXPLORATION: Solving an Equation by Graphing

Go to *BigIdeasMath.com* for an interactive tool to investigate this exploration.

Work with a partner. Solve $2x - 1 = -\frac{1}{2}x + 4$ by graphing.

   a.   Use the left side to write a linear equation. Then use the right side to write another linear equation.

   b.   Graph the two linear equations from part (a). Find the x-value of the point of intersection. Check that the x-value is the solution of

$$2x - 1 = -\frac{1}{2}x + 4.$$

   c.   Explain why this "graphical method" works.

---

2   EXPLORATION: Solving Equations Algebraically and Graphically

Go to *BigIdeasMath.com* for an interactive tool to investigate this exploration.

Work with a partner. Solve each equation using two methods.

   Method 1   Use an algebraic method.

   Method 2   Use a graphical method.

Is the solution the same using both methods?

   a. $\frac{1}{2}x + 4 = -\frac{1}{4}x + 1$ **b.** $\frac{2}{3}x + 4 = \frac{1}{3}x + 3$

5.5 Solving Equations by Graphing (continued)

2 **EXPLORATION:** Solving Equations Algebraically and Graphically (continued)

c. $-\frac{2}{3}x - 1 = \frac{1}{3}x - 4$

d. $\frac{4}{5}x + \frac{7}{5} = 3x - 3$

e. $-x + 2.5 = 2x - 0.5$

f. $-3x + 1.5 = x + 1.5$

Communicate Your Answer

3. How can you use a system of linear equations to solve an equation with variables on both sides?

4. Compare the algebraic method and the graphical method for solving a linear equation with variables on both sides. Describe the advantages and disadvantages of each method.

5.5 **Notetaking with Vocabulary**
For use after Lesson 5.5

In your own words, write the meaning of each vocabulary term.

absolute value equation

Core Concepts

Solving Linear Equations by Graphing

Step 1 To solve the equation $ax + b = cx + d$, write two linear equations.

$$ax + b = cx + d$$

$y = ax + b$ and $y = cx + d$

Step 2 Graph the system of linear equations. The x-value of the solution of the system of linear equations is the solution of the equation $ax + b = cx + d$.

Notes:

Name_____ Date _____

Extra Practice

In Exercises 1–9, solve the equation by graphing. Check your solution(s).

1. $2x - 7 = -2x + 9$

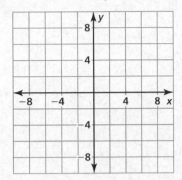

2. $3x = x - 4$

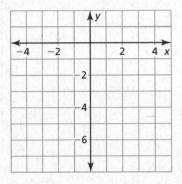

3. $4x + 1 = -2x - 5$

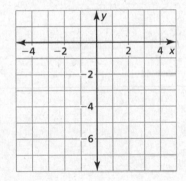

4. $-x - 4 = 3(x - 4)$

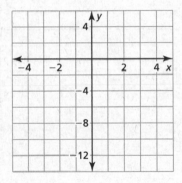

5. $-3x - 5 = 6 - 3x$

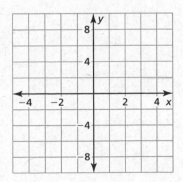

6. $7x - 14 = -7(2 - x)$

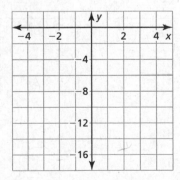

5.5 **Notetaking with Vocabulary** (continued)

7. $\left|3x\right| = \left|2x + 10\right|$

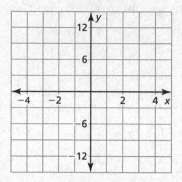

8. $\left|x - 1\right| = \left|x + 3\right|$

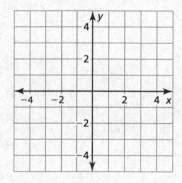 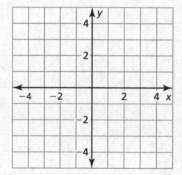

9. $\left|x + 4\right| = \left|2 - x\right|$

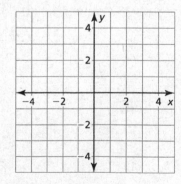 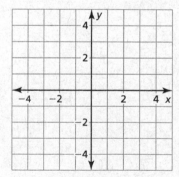

Graphing Linear Inequalities in Two Variables

For use with Exploration 5.6

Essential Question How can you graph a linear inequality in two variables?

> A **solution of a linear inequality in two variables** is an ordered pair (x, y) that makes the inequality true. The **graph of a linear inequality** in two variables shows all the solutions of the inequality in a coordinate plane.

---

1 EXPLORATION: Writing a Linear Inequality in Two Variables

Work with a partner.

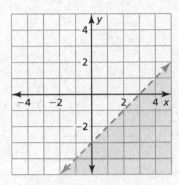

   a. Write an equation represented by the dashed line.

   b. The solutions of an inequality are represented by the shaded region. In words, describe the solutions of the inequality.

   c. Write an inequality represented by the graph. Which inequality symbol did you use? Explain your reasoning.

---

2 EXPLORATION: Using a Graphing Calculator

Go to *BigIdeasMath.com* for an interactive tool to investigate this exploration.

Work with a partner. Use a graphing calculator to graph $y \geq \frac{1}{4}x - 3$.

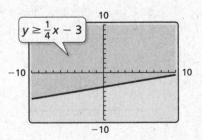

   a. Enter the equation $y = \frac{1}{4}x - 3$ into your calculator.

   b. The inequality has the symbol $\geq$. So, the region to be shaded is above the graph of $y = \frac{1}{4}x - 3$, as shown. Verify this by testing a point in this region, such as $(0, 0)$, to make sure it is a solution of the inequality.

Because the inequality symbol is *greater than or equal to*, the line is solid and not dashed. Some graphing calculators always use a solid line when graphing inequalities. In this case, you have to determine whether the line should be solid or dashed, based on the inequality symbol used in the original inequality.

5.6 Graphing Linear Inequalities in Two Variables (continued)

3 EXPLORATION: Graphing Linear Inequalities in Two Variables

Go to *BigIdeasMath.com* for an interactive tool to investigate this exploration.

Work with a partner. Graph each linear inequality in two variables. Explain your steps. Use a graphing calculator to check your graphs.

a. $y > x + 5$

b. $y \leq -\frac{1}{2}x + 1$

c. $y \geq -x - 5$

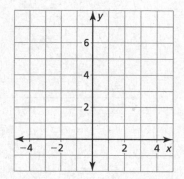
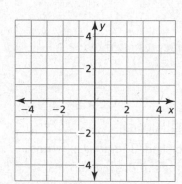
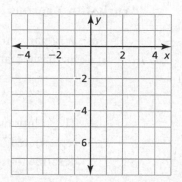

Communicate Your Answer

4. How can you graph a linear inequality in two variables?

5. Give an example of a real-life situation that can be modeled using a linear inequality in two variables.

5.6 Notetaking with Vocabulary
For use after Lesson 5.6

In your own words, write the meaning of each vocabulary term.

linear inequality in two variables

solution of a linear inequality in two variables

graph of a linear inequality

half-planes

Core Concepts

Graphing a Linear Inequality in Two Variables

Step 1 Graph the boundary line for the inequality. Use a dashed line for < or >.
Use a solid line for ≤ or ≥.

Step 2 Test a point that is not on the boundary line to determine whether it is a solution
of the inequality.

Step 3 When a test point is a solution, shade the half-plane that contains the point.
When the test point is *not* a solution, shade the half-plane that does *not* contain
the point.

Notes:

5.6 **Notetaking with Vocabulary** (continued)

Extra Practice

In Exercises 1–6, tell whether the ordered pair is a solution of the inequality.

1. $x + y > 5; (3, 2)$

2. $x - y \geq 2; (5, 3)$

3. $x + 2y \leq 4; (-1, 2)$

4. $5x + y < 7; (2, -2)$

5. $3x - 4y > 6; (-1, -1)$

6. $-x - 2y \geq 5; (-2, -3)$

In Exercises 7–18, graph the inequality in a coordinate plane.

7. $y < 4$

8. $y > -1$

9. $x > 3$

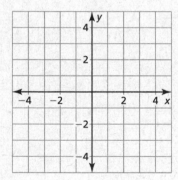
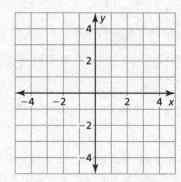
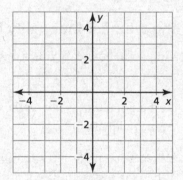

10. $x \leq -1$

11. $y < -2$

12. $x > -2$

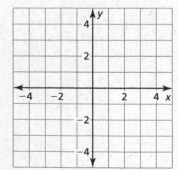
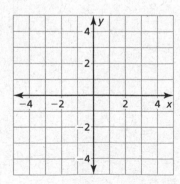
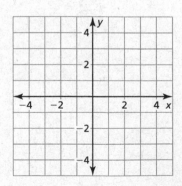

5.6 **Notetaking with Vocabulary** (continued)

13. $y < 3x + 1$

14. $y \geq -x + 1$

15. $x - y < 2$

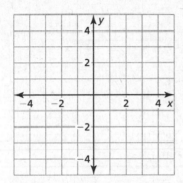 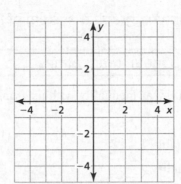 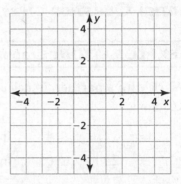

16. $x + y \geq -3$

17. $x + 2y < 4$

18. $-2x + 3y > 6$

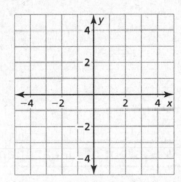 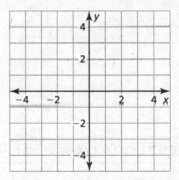

19. An online store sells digital cameras and cell phones. The store makes a $100 profit on the sale of each digital camera x and a $50 profit on the sale of each cell phone y. The store wants to make a profit of at least $300 from its sales of digital cameras and cell phones. Write and graph an inequality that represents how many digital cameras and cell phones they must sell. Identify and interpret two solutions of the inequality.

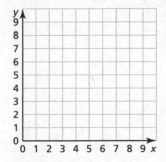

5.7 Systems of Linear Inequalities
For use with Exploration 5.7

Essential Question How can you graph a system of linear inequalities?

1 EXPLORATION: Graphing Linear Inequalities

Work with a partner. Match each linear inequality with its graph. Explain your reasoning.

$2x + y \leq 4$ Inequality 1

$2x - y \leq 0$ Inequality 2

A.

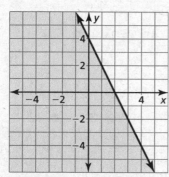

B.

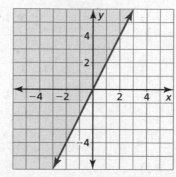

2 EXPLORATION: Graphing a System of Linear Inequalities

Go to *BigIdeasMath.com* **for an interactive tool to investigate this exploration.**

Work with a partner. Consider the linear inequalities given in Exploration 1.

$2x + y \leq 4$ Inequality 1

$2x - y \leq 0$ Inequality 2

a. Use two different colors to graph the inequalities in the same coordinate plane. What is the result?

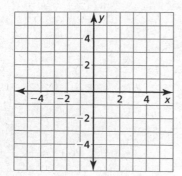

5.7 **Systems of Linear Inequalities** (continued)

---

2 **EXPLORATION:** Graphing a System of Linear Inequalities (continued)

    b. Describe each of the shaded regions of the graph. What does the unshaded region represent?

Communicate Your Answer

    3. How can you graph a system of linear inequalities?

    4. When graphing a system of linear inequalities, which region represents the solution of the system?

    5. Do you think all systems of linear inequalities have a solution? Explain your reasoning.

    6. Write a system of linear inequalities represented by the graph.

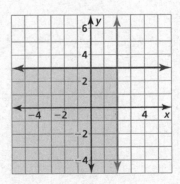

5.7 Notetaking with Vocabulary
For use after Lesson 5.7

In your own words, write the meaning of each vocabulary term.

system of linear inequalities

solution of a system of linear inequalities

graph of a system of linear inequalities

Core Concepts

Graphing a System of Linear Inequalities

Step 1 Graph each inequality in the same coordinate plane.

Step 2 Find the intersection of the half-planes that are solutions of the inequalities. This intersection is the graph of the system.

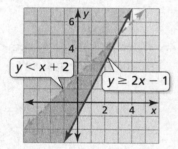

Notes:

5.7 Notetaking with Vocabulary (continued)

Extra Practice

In Exercises 1–4, tell whether the ordered pair is a solution of the system of linear inequalities.

1. $(0, 0); \; y > 2$
$\qquad y < x - 2$

2. $(-1, 1); \; y < 3$
$\qquad y > x - 4$

3. $(2, 3); \; y \geq x + 4$
$\qquad y \leq 2x + 4$

4. $(0, 4); \; y \leq -x + 4$
$\qquad y \geq 5x - 3$

In Exercises 5–8, graph the system of linear inequalities.

5. $y > -2$
$\quad y \leq 3x$

6. $y < 3$
$\quad x < 2$

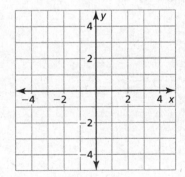

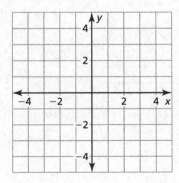

5.7 **Notetaking with Vocabulary** (continued)

7. $y \geq x - 2$

$y < -x + 2$

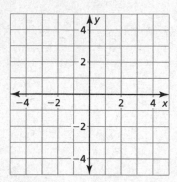

8. $2x + 3y < 6$

$y - 1 \geq -2x$

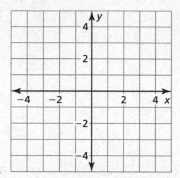

In Exercises 9–12, write a system of linear inequalities represented by the graph.

9.

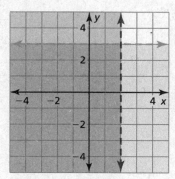

10.

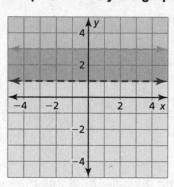

11.

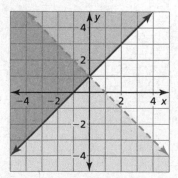

12.

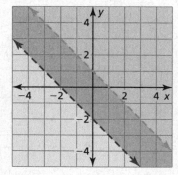

Name_____ Date_____

Evaluate the expression.

1. $(14 + 20 - 6) \div 4 - 6^2$ **2.** $(8 + 4)^2 + (13 - 10 \div 5)$ **3.** $8 \div 4 \cdot 19 + 18 + 13$

4. $3 \cdot 14 \cdot 11 + 4^2 + 19$ **5.** $(21 + 2)(14 - 6) + 3^2$ **6.** $7(3 \cdot 10 - 4^2) + 8$

Evaluate the expression.

7. 64^0 **8.** 4^{-2} **9.** $(-3)^{-3}$ **10.** $7^0 + 5^{-2}$

11. $(-2)^{-6} \cdot 8^0$ **12.** $7^3 \cdot 7^{-3}$ **13.** $10^2 \div (-5)^{-2}$ **14.** $6^{-2} \div 1^9 \cdot 9$

Write an equation for the *n*th term of the arithmetic sequence.

15. $1, 5, 9, 13, \ldots$ **16.** $21, 15, 9, 3, \ldots$ **17.** $-2, 1, 4, 7, \ldots$

18. $8, 6, 4, 2, \ldots$ **19.** $-10, -4, 2, 8, \ldots$ **20.** $16, 8, 0, -8, \ldots$

6.1 Exponential Functions
For use with Exploration 6.1

Essential Question What are some of the characteristics of the graph of an exponential function?

---

1 EXPLORATION: Exploring an Exponential Function

Work with a partner. Complete each table for the *exponential function* $y = 16(2)^x$. In each table, what do you notice about the values of x? What do you notice about the values of y?

x	$y = 16(2)^x$
0	
1	
2	
3	
4	
5	

x	$y = 16(2)^x$
0	
2	
4	
6	
8	
10	

---

2 EXPLORATION: Exploring an Exponential Function

Work with a partner. Repeat Exploration 1 for the exponential function $y = 16\left(\dfrac{1}{2}\right)^x$.

x	$y = 16\left(\dfrac{1}{2}\right)^x$
0	
1	
2	
3	
4	
5	

x	$y = 16\left(\dfrac{1}{2}\right)^x$
0	
2	
4	
6	
8	
10	

Do you think the statement below is true for *any* exponential function? Justify your answer.

"*As the independent variable x changes by a constant amount, the dependent variable y is multiplied by a constant factor.*"

6.1 Exponential Functions (continued)

3 **EXPLORATION:** Graphing Exponential Functions

Go to *BigIdeasMath.com* **for an interactive tool to investigate this exploration.**

Work with a partner. Sketch the graphs of the functions given in Explorations 1 and 2. How are the graphs similar? How are they different?

 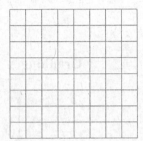

Communicate Your Answer

4. What are some of the characteristics of the graph of an exponential function?

5. Sketch the graph of each exponential function. Does each graph have the characteristics you described in Question 4? Explain your reasoning.

  a. $y = 2^x$ **b.** $y = 2(3)^x$ **c.** $y = 3(1.5)^x$

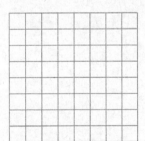 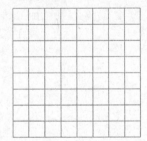 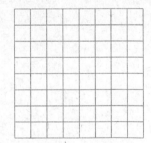

  d. $y = \left(\dfrac{1}{2}\right)^x$ **e.** $y = 3\left(\dfrac{1}{2}\right)^x$ **f.** $y = 2\left(\dfrac{3}{4}\right)^x$

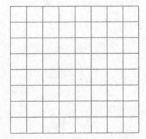 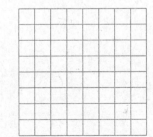 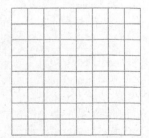

6.1 Notetaking with Vocabulary
For use after Lesson 6.1

In your own words, write the meaning of each vocabulary term.

exponential function

Core Concepts

Graphing $y = ab^x$ **When** $b > 1$

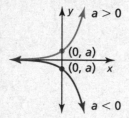

Graphing $y = ab^x$ **When** $0 < b < 1$

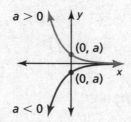

Notes:

Name_____ Date _____

Extra Practice

In Exercises 1–4, determine whether the table represents an exponential function. Explain.

1.

x	y
1	8
2	4
3	2
4	1

2.

x	y
1	3
2	7
3	11
4	15

3.

x	y
−1	12
0	9
1	6
2	3

4.

x	y
−1	0.125
0	0.5
1	2
2	8

In Exercises 5–7, evaluate the function for the given value of x.

5. $y = 3^x; x = 5$

6. $y = \left(\frac{1}{4}\right)^x; x = 3$

7. $y = 3(4)^x; x = 4$

In Exercises 8 and 9, graph the function. Compare the graph to the graph of the parent function. Describe the domain and range of f.

8. $f(x) = -2^x$

9. $f(x) = 2\left(\frac{1}{4}\right)^x$

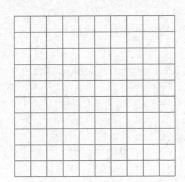

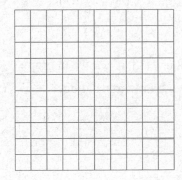

6.1 **Notetaking with Vocabulary** (continued)

In Exercises 10 and 11, graph the function. Describe the domain and range.

10. $f(x) = 4^x - 2$

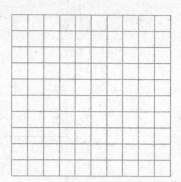

11. $f(x) = 4\left(\dfrac{1}{2}\right)^{x+1}$

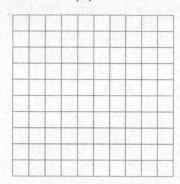

In Exercises 12 and 13, write an exponential function represented by the table or graph.

12.

x	0	1	2	3
f(x)	3	18	108	648

13.

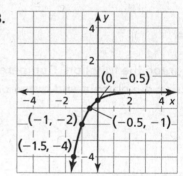

14. Graph the function $f(x) = 2^x$. Then graph $g(x) = 2^x + 3$. How are the y-intercept, domain, and range affected by the translation?

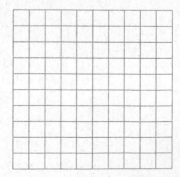

6.2 **Exponential Growth and Decay**
For use with Exploration 6.2

Essential Question What are some of the characteristics of exponential growth and exponential decay functions?

1 EXPLORATION: Predicting a Future Event

Work with a partner. It is estimated, that in 1782, there were about 100,000 nesting pairs of bald eagles in the United States. By the 1960s, this number had dropped to about 500 nesting pairs. In 1967, the bald eagle was declared an endangered species in the United States. With protection, the nesting pair population began to increase. Finally, in 2007, the bald eagle was removed from the list of endangered and threatened species.

Describe the pattern shown in the graph. Is it exponential growth? Assume the pattern continues. When will the population return to that of the late 1700s? Explain your reasoning.

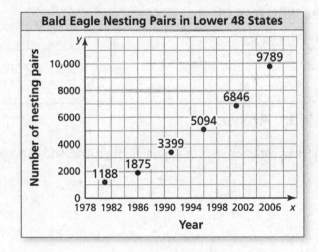

6.2 **Exponential Growth and Decay** (continued)

---

2 **EXPLORATION:** Describing a Decay Pattern

Work with a partner. A forensic pathologist was called to estimate the time of death of a person. At midnight, the body temperature was 80.5°F and the room temperature was a constant 60°F. One hour later, the body temperature was 78.5°F.

   a. By what percent did the difference between the body temperature and the room temperature drop during the hour?

   b. Assume that the original body temperature was 98.6°F. Use the percent decrease found in part (a) to make a table showing the decreases in body temperature. Use the table to estimate the time of death.

Time (*h*)									
Temperature difference (°F)									
Body temperature (°F)									

Communicate Your Answer

3. What are some of the characteristics of exponential growth and exponential decay functions?

4. Use the Internet or some other reference to find an example of each type of function. Your examples should be different than those given in Explorations 1 and 2.

   a. exponential growth

   b. exponential decay

6.2 Notetaking with Vocabulary
For use after Lesson 6.2

In your own words, write the meaning of each vocabulary term.

exponential growth

exponential growth function

exponential decay

exponential decay function

compound interest

Core Concepts

Exponential Growth Functions

A function of the form $y = a(1 + r)^t$, where $a > 0$ and $r > 0$, is an **exponential growth function**.

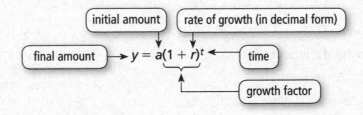

Notes:

6.2 **Notetaking with Vocabulary** (continued)

Exponential Decay Functions

A function of the form $y = a(1 - r)^t$, where $a > 0$ and $0 < r < 1$, is an **exponential decay function**.

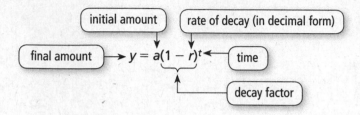

Notes:

Compound Interest

Compound interest is the interest earned on the principal *and* on previously earned interest. The balance y of an account earning compound interest is

$$y = P\left(1 + \frac{r}{n}\right)^{nt}.$$

P = principal (initial amount)

r = annual interest rate (in decimal form)

t = time (in years)

n = number of times interest is compounded per year

Notes:

6.2 **Notetaking with Vocabulary** (continued)

Extra Practice

1. In 2005, there were 100 rabbits in Polygon Park. The population increased by 11% each year.

    a. Write an exponential growth function that represents the population t years after 2005.

    b. What will the population be in 2025? Round your answer to the nearest whole number.

In Exercises 2–5, determine whether the table represents an *exponential growth* function, an *exponential decay function*, or *neither*. Explain.

2.

x	y
0	20
1	30
2	45
3	67.5

3.

x	y
−1	160
0	40
1	10
2	2.5

4.

x	y
1	32
2	22
3	12
4	2

5.

x	y
−1	4
0	10
1	25
2	62.5

In Exercises 6–8, determine whether each function represents *exponential growth* or *exponential decay*. Identify the percent rate of change.

6. $y = 4(0.95)^t$

7. $y = 500(1.08)^t$

8. $w(t) = \left(\dfrac{3}{4}\right)^t$

In Exercises 9 and 10, write a function that represents the balance after t years.

9. $3000 deposit that earns 6% annual interest compounded quarterly.

10. $5000 deposit that earns 7.2% annual interest compounded monthly.

6.3 Comparing Linear and Exponential Functions
For use with Exploration 6.3

Essential Question How can you compare the growth rates of linear and exponential functions?

1 EXPLORATION: Comparing Values

Work with a partner. An art collector buys two paintings. The value of each painting after t year is y dollars. Complete each table. Compare the values of the two paintings. Which painting's value has a constant growth rate? Which painting's value has an increasing growth rate? Explain your reasoning.

t	$y = 19t + 5$
0	
1	
2	
3	
4	

t	$y = 3^t$
0	
1	
2	
3	
4	

6.3 **Comparing Linear and Exponential Functions** (continued)

2 **EXPLORATION:** Comparing Values

Work with a partner. Analyze the values of the two paintings over the given time periods. The value of each painting after t years is y dollars. Which painting's value eventually overtakes the other?

t	$y = 19t + 5$
4	
5	
6	
7	
8	
9	

t	$y = 3^t$
4	
5	
6	
7	
8	
9	

3 **EXPLORATION:** Comparing Graphs

Work with a partner. Use the tables in Explorations 1 and 2 to graph $y = 19t + 5$ and $y = 3^t$ in the same coordinate plane. Compares the graph of the functions.

Communicate Your Answer

3. How can you compare the growth rates of linear and exponential functions?

4. Which function has a growth rate that is eventually much greater than the growth rates of the other function? Explain your reasoning.

6.3 Notetaking with Vocabulary
For use after Lesson 6.3

In your own words, write the meaning of each vocabulary term.

average rate of change

Core Concepts

Linear and Exponential Functions

Linear Function

$$y = mx + b$$

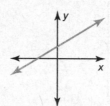

Exponential Function

$$y = ab^x$$

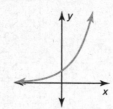

Notes:

Differences and Ratios of Functions

You can use patterns between consecutive data pairs to determine which type of function models the data.

- **Linear Function** The differences of consecutive y-values are constant.

- **Exponential Function** Consecutive y-values have a common *ratio*.

In each case, the differences of consecutive x-values need to be constant.

Notes:

\Name _____ Date _____

Comparing Functions Using Average Rates of Change

As a and b increase, the average rate of change between $x = a$ and $x = b$ of an increasing exponential function $y = f(x)$ will eventually exceed the average rate of change between $x = a$ and $x = b$ of an increasing linear function $y = g(x)$. So, as x increases, $f(x)$ will eventually exceed $g(x)$.

Notes:

Extra Practice

In Exercises 1–4, plot the points. Tell whether the points appear to represent a *linear function*, **an** *exponential function*, **or** *neither*.

1. $(-3, 2), (-2, 4), (-4, 4), (-1, 8), (-5, 8)$ **2.** $(-3, 1), (-2, 2), (-1, 4), (0, 8), (2, 14)$

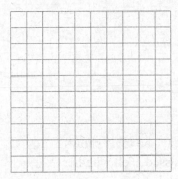 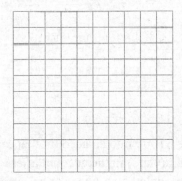

3. $(4, 0), (2, 1), (0, 3), (-1, 6), (-2, 10)$ **4.** $(2, -4), (0, -2), (-2, 0), (-4, 2), (-6, 4)$

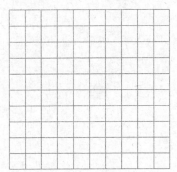 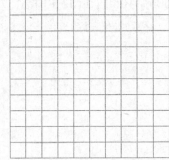

6.3 Notetaking with Vocabulary (continued)

In Exercises 5 and 6, tell whether the table of values represents a *linear*, or an *exponential* function.

5.

x	−2	−1	0	1	2
y	7	4	1	−2	−5

6.

x	−2	−1	0	1	2
y	$\frac{1}{18}$	$\frac{1}{3}$	2	12	72

In Exercises 7 and 8, tell whether the data represent a *linear*, or an *exponential* function. Then write the function.

7. $(-2, -4), (-1, -1), (0, 2), (1, 5), (2, 8)$

8. $(-2, 1.75), (-1, 3.5), (0, 7), (1, 14), (2, 28)$

9. A person invests $1000 into an account that earns compound interest. The table shows the amount A (in dollars) in the account after t (in years) time has passed. Tell whether the data can be modeled by a *linear* or an *exponential* function. Explain.

Time, t	0	1	2	3	4
Amount, A	1000	1050	1102.50	1157.63	1215.51

6.4 Solving Exponential Equations
For use with Exploration 6.4

Essential Question How can you solve an exponential equation graphically?

1 EXPLORATION: Solving an Exponential Equation Graphically

Go to *BigIdeasMath.com* for an interactive tool to investigate this exploration.

Work with a partner. Use a graphing calculator to solve the exponential equation $2.5^{x-3} = 6.25$ graphically. Describe your process and explain how you determined the solution.

2 EXPLORATION: The Number of Solutions of an Exponential Equation

Go to *BigIdeasMath.com* for an interactive tool to investigate this exploration.

Work with a partner.

a. Use a graphing calculator to graph the equation $y = 2^x$.

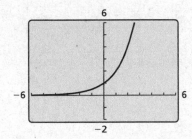

b. In the same viewing window, graph a linear equation (if possible) that does not intersect the graph of $y = 2^x$.

c. In the same viewing window, graph a linear equation (if possible) that intersects the graph of $y = 2^x$ in more than one point.

d. Is it possible for an exponential equation to have no solution? more than one solution? Explain your reasoning.

6.4 Solving Exponential Equations (continued)

---

3 **EXPLORATION:** Solving Exponential Equations Graphically

Go to *BigIdeasMath.com* for an interactive tool to investigate this exploration.

Work with a partner. Use a graphing calculator to solve each equation.

a. $2^x = \dfrac{1}{2}$

b. $2^{x+1} = 0$

c. $2^x = 1$

d. $3^x = 9$

e. $3^{x-1} = 0$

f. $4^{2x} = \dfrac{1}{16}$

g. $2^{3x} = \dfrac{1}{8}$

h. $3^{x+2} = \dfrac{1}{9}$

i. $2^{x-2} = \dfrac{3}{2}x - 2$

Communicate Your Answer

4. How can you solve an exponential equation graphically?

5. A population of 30 mice is expected to double each year. The number p of mice in the population each year is given by $p = 30(2^n)$. In how many years will there be 960 mice in the population?

6.4 Notetaking with Vocabulary
For use after Lesson 6.4

In your own words, write the meaning of each vocabulary term.

exponential equation

Core Concepts

Property of Equality for Exponential Equations

Words   Two powers with the *same positive base b*, where $b \neq 1$, are equal if and only if their exponents are equal.

Numbers   If $2^x = 2^5$, then $x = 5$. If $x = 5$, then $2^x = 2^5$.

Algebra   If $b > 0$ and $b \neq 1$, then $b^x = b^y$ if and only if $x = y$.

Notes:

Name_____ Date _____

6.4 **Notetaking with Vocabulary** (continued)

Extra Practice

In Exercises 1–15, solve the equation. Check your solution.

1. $3^{4x} = 3^{12}$

2. $8^{x+5} = 8^{20}$

3. $6^{4x-5} = 6^{2x}$

4. $5^{6x-3} = 5^{-3+4x}$

5. $4^{2x+11} = 1024$

6. $8^{3-2x} = 512$

7. $4^{7-x} = 256$

8. $49^{x-2} = 343$

9. $36^{6x-1} = 6^{5x}$

10. $9^{x-4} = 81^{3x}$

11. $64^{x+1} = 512^x$

12. $6^{2x} = 36^{2x+1}$

6.4 Notetaking with Vocabulary (continued)

13. $\left(\frac{1}{7}\right)^x = 2401$　　　　**14.** $\frac{1}{512} = 2^{3x-1}$　　　　**15.** $25^{2-2x} = \left(\frac{1}{625}\right)^{x+1}$

In Exercises 16–21, use a graphing calculator to solve the equation.

16. $3^{x+3} = 9$　　　　**17.** $\left(\frac{1}{4}\right)^{-x-1} = 64$　　　　**18.** $-2x - 2 = -2^{-x+1}$

19. $2^{x+2} = 5^{x+2}$　　　　**20.** $7^{-x+1} = 4^{x-1}$　　　　**21.** $-\frac{1}{2}x - 3 = \left(\frac{2}{3}\right)^{2x-1}$

22. You deposit $1000 in a savings account that earns 5% annual interest compounded yearly.

　　a. Write an exponential equation to determine when the balance of the account will be $1500.

　　b. Solve the equation.

6.5 Geometric Sequences
For use with Exploration 6.5

Essential Question How can you use a geometric sequence to describe a pattern?

In a **geometric sequence**, the ratio between each pair of consecutive terms is the same. This ratio is called the **common ratio**.

1 EXPLORATION: Describing Calculator Patterns

Work with a partner. Enter the keystrokes on a calculator and record the results in the table. Describe the pattern.

a. Step 1 [2] [=]

   Step 2 [×] [2] [=]

   Step 3 [×] [2] [=]

   Step 4 [×] [2] [=]

   Step 5 [×] [2] [=]

b. Step 1 [6] [4] [=]

   Step 2 [×] [.] [5] [=]

   Step 3 [×] [.] [5] [=]

   Step 4 [×] [.] [5] [=]

   Step 5 [×] [.] [5] [=]

Step	1	2	3	4	5
Calculator display					

Step	1	2	3	4	5
Calculator display					

c. Use a calculator to make your own sequence. Start with any number and multiply by 3 each time. Record your results in the table.

Step	1	2	3	4	5
Calculator display					

d. Part (a) involves a geometric sequence with a common ratio of 2. What is the common ratio in part (b)? part (c)?

6.5 **Geometric Sequences** (continued)

2 **EXPLORATION:** Folding a Sheet of Paper

Work with a partner. A sheet of paper is about 0.1 millimeter thick.

    a. How thick will it be when you fold it in half once? twice? three times?

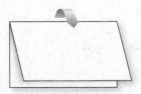

    b. What is the greatest number of times you can fold a piece of paper in half? How thick is the result?

    c. Do you agree with the statement below? Explain your reasoning.

    "If it were possible to fold the paper in half 15 times, it would be taller than you."

Communicate Your Answer

3. How can you use a geometric sequence to describe a pattern?

4. Give an example of a geometric sequence from real life other than paper folding.

6.5 Notetaking with Vocabulary
For use after Lesson 6.5

In your own words, write the meaning of each vocabulary term.

geometric sequence

common ratio

Core Concepts

Geometric Sequence

In a **geometric sequence**, the ratio between each pair of consecutive terms is the same. This ratio is called the **common ratio**. Each term is found by multiplying the previous term by the common ratio.

$$1, \quad 5, \quad 25, \quad 125, \ldots \quad \text{Terms of a geometric sequence}$$
$$\times 5 \quad \times 5 \quad \times 5 \leftarrow \boxed{\text{common ratio}}$$

Notes:

Equation for a Geometric Sequence

Let a_n be the nth term of a geometric sequence with first term a_1 and common ratio r. The nth term is given by

$$a_n = a_1 r^{n-1}.$$

Notes:

Name_____ Date_____

Extra Practice

In Exercises 1–6, determine whether the sequence is *arithmetic, geometric,* or *neither*. Explain your reasoning.

1. $1, -4, 16, -64, \ldots$ **2.** $3, 7, 11, 15, \ldots$ **3.** $2, 4, 8, 32, \ldots$

4. $12, 9, 7, 5, \ldots$ **5.** $6, 18, 54, 162, \ldots$ **6.** $11, 19, 27, 35, \ldots$

In Exercises 7–9, write the next three terms of the geometric sequence.

7. $7, 21, 63, 189, \ldots$ **8.** $576, 288, 144, 72, \ldots$ **9.** $5, -10, 20, -40, \ldots$

In Exercises 10–12, write the next three terms of the geometric sequence. Then graph the sequence.

10. $12, 6, 3, \dfrac{3}{2}, \ldots$ **11.** $3, 12, 48, 192, \ldots$ **12.** $0.008, 0.04, 0.2, 1, \ldots$

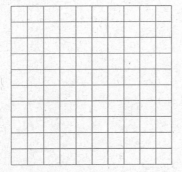 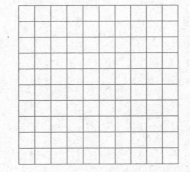 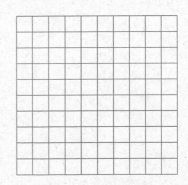

Name_____ Date _____

In Exercises 13–20, write an equation for the *n*th term of the geometric sequence.
Then find a_6.

13. $6561, 2187, 729, 243, \ldots$ **14.** $8, -24, 72, -216, \ldots$ **15.** $3, 15, 75, 375, \ldots$

16.

n	1	2	3	4
a_n	2916	972	324	108

17.

n	1	2	3	4
a_n	11	44	176	704

18.

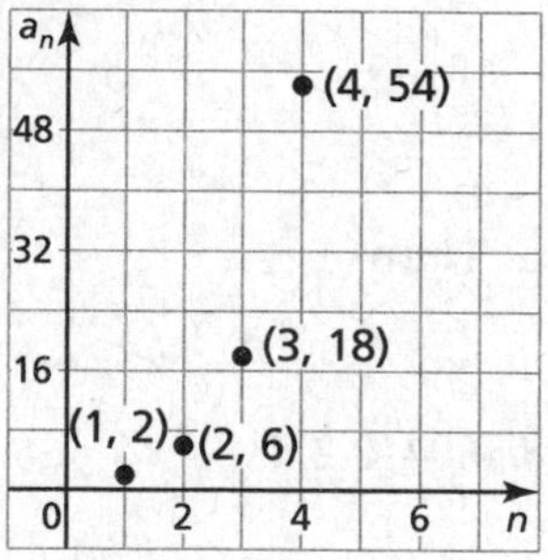

19.

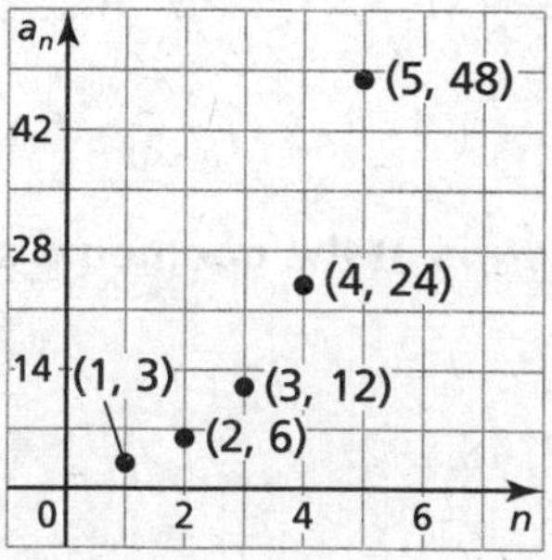

20.

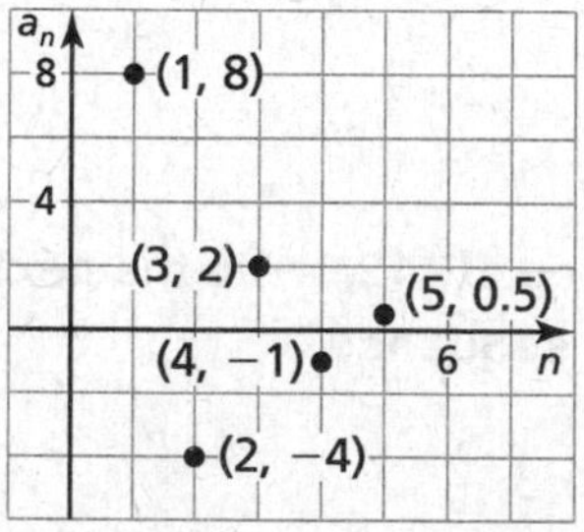

6.6 Recursively Defined Sequences
For use with Exploration 6.6

Essential Question How can you define a sequence recursively?

A **recursive rule** gives the beginning term(s) of a sequence and a *recursive equation* that tells how a_n is related to one or more preceding terms

1 EXPLORATION: Describing a Pattern

Work with a partner. Consider a hypothetical population of rabbits. Start with one breeding pair. After each month, each breeding pair produces another breeding pair. The total number of rabbits each month follows the exponential pattern 2, 4, 8, 16, 32, …. Now suppose that in the first month after each pair is born, the pair is too young to reproduce. Each pair produces another pair after it is 2 months old. Find the total number of pairs in months 6, 7, and 8.

Month		Number of pairs
1	Red pair is too young to produce.	1
2	Red pair produces blue pair.	1
3	Red pair produces green pair.	2
4	Red pair produces orange pair. / Blue pair produces purple pair.	3
5		5
6		
7		
8		

6.6 Recursively Defined Sequences (continued)

2 EXPLORATION: Using a Recursive Equation

Work with a partner. Consider the following recursive equation.

$$a_n = a_{n-1} + a_{n-2}$$

Each term in the sequence is the sum of the two preceding terms.

Complete the table. Compare the results with the sequence of the number of pairs in Exploration 1.

a_1	a_2	a_3	a_4	a_5	a_6	a_7	a_8
1	1						

Communicate Your Answer

3. How can you define a sequence recursively?

4. Use the Internet or some other reference to determine the mathematician who first described the sequences in Explorations 1 and 2.

Notetaking with Vocabulary
For use after Lesson 6.6

In your own words, write the meaning of each vocabulary term.

explicit rule

recursive rule

Core Concepts

Recursive Equation for an Arithmetic Sequence

$a_n = a_{n-1} + d$, where d is the common difference

Recursive Equation for a Geometric Sequence

$a_n = r \bullet a_{n-1}$, where r is the common ratio

Notes:

6.6   **Notetaking with Vocabulary** (continued)

Extra Practice

In Exercises 1–6, write the first six terms of the sequence. Then graph the sequence.

1. $a_1 = -2; a_n = -2a_{n-1}$ **2.** $a_1 = -4; a_n = a_{n-1} + 3$ **3.** $a_1 = 4; a_n = 1.5a_{n-1}$

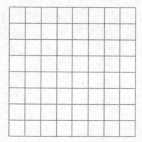 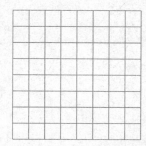 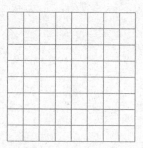

4. $a_1 = 14; a_n = a_{n-1} - 4$ **5.** $a_1 = -\dfrac{1}{2}; a_n = -2a_{n-1}$ **6.** $a_1 = -3; a_n = a_{n-1} + 2$

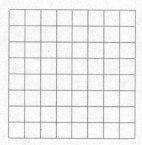 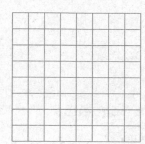 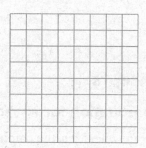

In Exercises 7 and 8, write a recursive rule for the sequence.

7.

n	1	2	3	4
a_n	324	108	36	12

8.

n	1	2	3	4
a_n	9	14	19	24

6.6 **Notetaking with Vocabulary** (continued)

In Exercises 9–13, write a recursive rule for the sequence.

9. $3125, 625, 125, 25, \ldots$ **10.** $8, -24, 72, -216, \ldots$ **11.** $7, 13, 19, 25, \ldots$

12.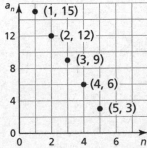

13.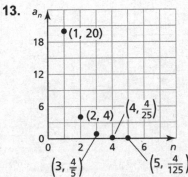

In Exercises 14–16, write an explicit rule for the recursive rule.

14. $a_1 = 4; a_n = 3a_{n-1}$ **15.** $a_1 = 6; a_n = a_{n-1} + 11$ **16.** $a_1 = -1; a_n = 5a_{n-1}$

In Exercises 17–19, write a recursive rule for the explicit rule.

17. $a_n = 6n + 2$ **18.** $a_n = (-3)^{n-1}$ **19.** $a_n = -2n + 1$

In Exercises 20–22, write a recursive rule for the sequence. Then write the next two terms of the sequence.

20. $2, 4, 6, 10, 16, 26, \ldots$ **21.** $1, 3, -2, 5, -7, 12, \ldots$ **22.** $1, 2, 2, 4, 8, 32, \ldots$

Chapter 7 Maintaining Mathematical Proficiency

The table shows the results of a survey. Display the data in a histogram.

1.

Movies attended last month	Frequency
0–1	16
2–3	12
4–5	8

2.

Hours of homework	Frequency
0–1	8
2–3	15
4–5	4
6–7	1

The table shows the results of a survey. Display the data in a circle graph.

3.

Favorite ice cream flavor	Vanilla	Chocolate	Strawberry	Butter Pecan
Students	5	6	4	3

4.

Favorite Sport	Baseball	Tennis	Basketball	Soccer	Golf
Students	10	4	8	7	2

7.1 Measures of Center and Variation
For use with Exploration 7.1

Essential Question How can you describe the variation of a data set?

---

1 EXPLORATION: Describing the Variation of Data

Work with a partner. The graphs show the weights of the players on a professional football team and a professional baseball team.

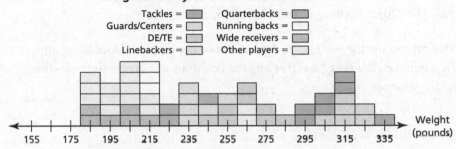

Weights of Players on a Football Team

Tackles = ▨ Quarterbacks = ▨
Guards/Centers = ▨ Running backs = ▢
DE/TE = ▨ Wide receivers = ▨
Linebackers = ▨ Other players = ▢

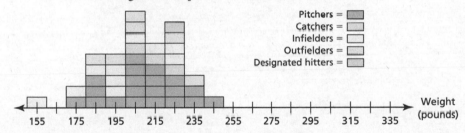

Weights of Players on a Baseball Team

Pitchers = ▨
Catchers = ▨
Infielders = ▢
Outfielders = ▢
Designated hitters = ▨

a. Describe the data in each graph in terms of how much the weights vary from the mean. Explain your reasoning.

b. Compare how much the weights of the players on the football team vary from the mean to how much the weights of the players on the baseball team vary from the mean.

c. Does there appear to be a correlation between the body weights and the positions of players in professional football? in professional baseball? Explain.

7.1   **Measures of Center and Variation** (continued)

---

2   **EXPLORATION:** Describing the Variation of Data

Go to *BigIdeasMath.com* for an interactive tool to investigate this exploration.

Work with a partner. The weights (in pounds) of the players on a professional basketball team by position are as follows.

Power forwards: 235, 255, 295, 245; small forwards: 235, 235; centers: 255, 245, 325; point guards: 205, 185, 205; shooting guards: 205, 215, 185.

Make a graph that represents the weights and positions of the players. Does there appear to be a correlation between the body weights and the positions of players in professional basketball? Explain your reasoning

Communicate Your Answer

3. How can you describe the variation of a data set?

Name_____ Date_____

7.1 Notetaking with Vocabulary
For use after Lesson 7.1

In your own words, write the meaning of each vocabulary term.

measure of center

mean

median

mode

outlier

measure of variation

range

standard deviation

data transformation

Notes:

7.1 Notetaking with Vocabulary (continued)

Core Concepts

Mean

The **mean** of a numerical data set is the sum of the data divided by the number of data values. The symbol $\bar{x}$ represents the mean. It is read as "x-bar."

Median

The **median** of a numerical data set is the middle number when the values are written in numerical order. When a data set has an even number of values, the median is the mean of the two middle values.

Mode

The **mode** of a data set is the value or values that occur most often. There may be one mode, no mode, or more than one mode.

Notes:

Standard Deviation

The **standard deviation** of a numerical data set is a measure of how much a typical value in the data set differs from the mean. The symbol σ represents the standard deviation. It is read as "sigma." It is given by

$$\sigma = \sqrt{\frac{(x_1 - \bar{x})^2 + (x_2 - \bar{x})^2 + \cdots + (x_n - \bar{x})^2}{n}}$$

where n is the number of values in the data set. The deviation of a data value x is the difference of the data value and the mean of the data set, $x - \bar{x}$.

Step 1 Find the mean, $\bar{x}$.

Step 2 Find the deviation of each data value, $x - \bar{x}$.

Step 3 Square each deviation, $(x - \bar{x})^2$.

Step 4 Find the mean of the squared deviations. This is called the *variance*.

Step 5 Take the square root of the variance.

Notes:

7.1 **Notetaking with Vocabulary** (continued)

Data Transformations Using Addition

When a real number k is added to each value in a numerical data set

- the measures of center of the new data set can be found by adding k to the original measures of center.

- the measures of variation of the new data set are the *same* as the original measures of variation.

Data Transformations Using Multiplication

When each value in a numerical data set is multiplied by a real number k, where $k > 0$, the measures of center and variation can be found by multiplying the original measures by k.

Notes:

Extra Practice

1. Consider the data set: 2, 5, 16, 2, 2, 7, 3, 4, 4.

   a. Find the mean, median, and mode of the data set.

   b. Determine which measure of center best represents the data. Explain.

2. The table shows the masses of eight gorillas.

Masses (kilograms)							
160	157	162	158	44	160	159	161

   a. Identify the outlier. How does the outlier affect the mean, median, and mode?

   b. Describe one possible explanation for the outlier.

7.1 **Notetaking with Vocabulary** (continued)

3. The heights of the members of two girls' basketball teams are shown. Find the range of the heights for each team. Compare your results.

Team A Heights (inches)									
58	75	60	48	56	78	60	57	54	59

Team B Heights (inches)									
49	50	70	56	58	66	64	57	62	63

4. Consider the data in Exercise 3.

   a. Find the standard deviation of the heights of Team A. Interpret your result.

   b. Find the standard deviation of the heights of Team B. Interpret your result.

   c. Compare the standard deviations for Team A and Team B. What can you conclude?

5. Find the values of the measures shown when each value in the data set increases by 8.

   Mean: 42   Median: 40   Mode: 38
   Range: 15   Standard deviation: 4.9

7.2 Box-and-Whisker Plots

For use with Exploration 7.2

Essential Question How can you use a box-and-whisker plot to describe a data set?

---

1 **EXPLORATION:** Drawing a Box-and-Whisker Plot

Go to *BigIdeasMath.com* for an interactive tool to investigate this exploration.

Work with a partner. The numbers of first cousins of the students in a ninth-grade class are shown. A *box-and-whisker plot* is one way to represent the data visually.

Numbers of First Cousins			
3	10	18	8
9	3	0	32
23	19	13	8
6	3	3	10
12	45	1	5
13	24	16	14

a. Order the data on a strip of grid paper with 24 equally spaced boxes.

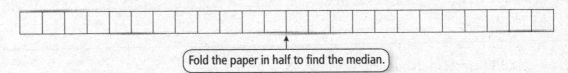

Fold the paper in half to find the median.

b. Fold the paper in half again to divide the data into four groups. Because there are 24 numbers in the data set, each group should have 6 numbers. Find the least value, the greatest value, the first quartile, and the third quartile.

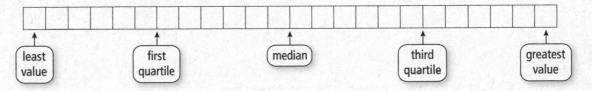

least value   first quartile   median   third quartile   greatest value

---

7.2 **Box-and-Whisker Plots** (continued)

1 **EXPLORATION:** Drawing a Box-and-Whisker Plot (continued)

c. Explain how the box-and-whisker plot shown represents the data set.

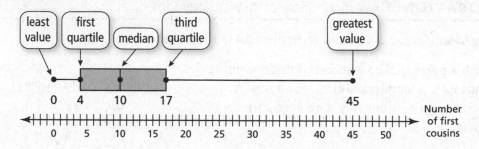

Communicate Your Answer

2. How can you use a box-and-whisker plot to describe a data set?

3. Interpret each box-and-whisker plot.

a. body mass indices (BMI) of students in a ninth-grade class

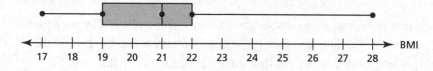

b. heights of roller coasters at an amusement park

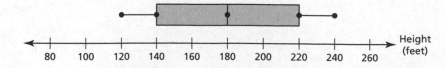

Notetaking with Vocabulary
For use after Lesson 7.2

In your own words, write the meaning of each vocabulary term.

box-and-whisker plot

quartile

five-number summary

interquartile range

Core Concepts

Box-and-Whisker Plot

A **box-and-whisker plot** shows the variability of a data set along a number line using the least value, the greatest value, and the *quartiles* of the data. **Quartiles** divide the data set into four equal parts. The median (second quartile, Q2) divides the data set into two halves. The median of the lower half is the first quartile, Q1. The median of the upper half is the third quartile, Q3.

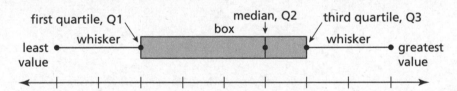

The five numbers that make up a box-and-whisker plot are called the **five-number summary** of the data set.

Notes:

7.2   **Notetaking with Vocabulary** (continued)

Shapes of Box-and-Whisker Plots

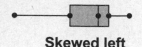
Skewed left

- The left whisker is longer than the right whisker.

- Most of the data are on the right side of the plot.

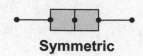
Symmetric

- The whiskers are about the same length.

- The median is in the middle of the plot.

Skewed right

- The right whisker is longer than the left whisker.

- Most of the data are on the left side of the plot.

Notes:

Extra Practice

In Exercises 1 and 2, make a box-and-whisker plot that represents the data.

1. Hours of sleep: 7, 9, 8, 8, 8, 6, 6, 5, 4

2. Algebra test scores: 71, 92, 84, 76, 88, 96, 84, 63, 82

7.2 **Notetaking with Vocabulary (continued)**

3. The box-and-whisker plot represents the prices (in dollars) of soccer balls at different sporting goods stores.

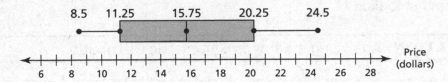

8.5   11.25   15.75   20.25   24.5

Price (dollars)

a. Find and interpret the range of the data.

b. Describe the distribution of the data.

c. Find and interpret the interquartile range of the data.

d. Are the data more spread out below Q1 or above Q3? Explain.

4. The double box-and-whisker plot represents the number of tornados per month for a year for two states.

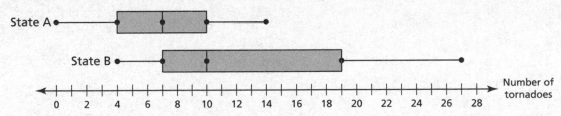

State A

State B

Number of tornadoes

a. Identify the shape of each distribution.

b. Which state's tornadoes are more spread out? Explain.

c. Which state had the single least number of tornadoes in a month during the year? Explain.

7.3 Shapes of Distributions
For use with Exploration 7.3

Essential Question   How can you use a histogram to characterize the basic shape of a distribution?

---

1 | **EXPLORATION:** Analyzing a Famous Symmetric Distribution

Work with a partner. A famous data set was collected in Scotland in the mid-1800s. It contains the chest sizes, measured in inches, of 5738 men in the Scottish Militia. Estimate the percent of the chest sizes that lie within (a) 1 standard deviation of the mean, (b) 2 standard deviations of the mean, and (c) 3 standard deviations of the mean. Explain your reasoning.

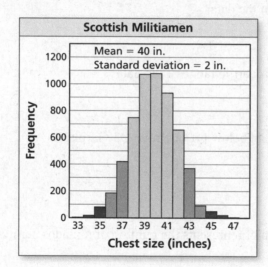

Name_____ Date_____

2 **EXPLORATION:** Comparing Two Symmetric Distributions

Work with a partner. The graphs show the distributions of the heights of 250 adult American males and 250 adult American females.

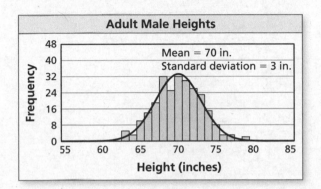

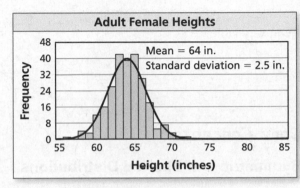

a. Which data set has a smaller standard deviation? Explain what this means in the context of the problem.

b. Estimate the percent of male heights between 67 inches and 73 inches.

Communicate Your Answer

3. How can you use a histogram to characterize the basic shape of a distribution?

4. All three distributions in Explorations 1 and 2 are roughly symmetric. The histograms are called "bell-shaped."

a. What are the characteristics of a symmetric distribution?

b. Why is a symmetric distribution called "bell-shaped?"

c. Give two other real-life examples of symmetric distributions.

7.3 Notetaking with Vocabulary
For use after Lesson 7.3

In your own words, write the meaning of each vocabulary term.

histogram

frequency table

Core Concepts

Symmetric and Skewed Distributions

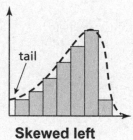

Skewed left

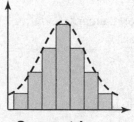

Symmetric

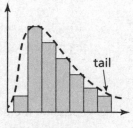

Skewed right

- The "tail" of the graph extends to the left.
- Most of the data are on the right.

- The data on the right of the distribution are approximately a mirror image of the data on the left of the distribution.

- The "tail" of the graph extends to the right.
- Most of the data are on the left.

Notes:

7.3 **Notetaking with Vocabulary** (continued)

Choosing Appropriate Measures

When a data distribution is symmetric,

- use the mean to describe the center and

- use the standard deviation to describe the variation.

When a data distribution is skewed,

- use the median to describe the center and

- use the five-number summary to describe the variation.

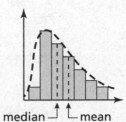

Notes:

Extra Practice

1. The table shows the average annual snowfall (in inches) of 26 cities.

   a. Display the data in a histogram using six intervals beginning with 15–28.

Average Annual Snowfall (inches)		
22	68	33
15	28	31
20	18	30
15	54	16
44	43	17
95	41	30
29	23	47
37	26	54
16	30	

   b. Which measures of center and variation best represent the data? Explain.

   c. A weather station lists the top 20 snowiest major cities. The city in 20th place had 51 inches of snow. How would you interpret the data?

7.3 **Notetaking with Vocabulary** (continued)

2. The double histogram shows the distributions of monthly precipitation for two towns over a 50-month period. Compare the distributions using their shapes and appropriate measures of center and variation.

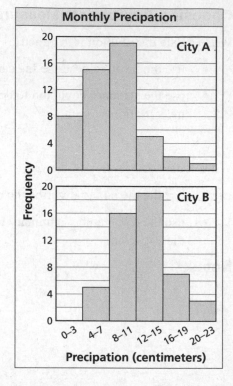

Monthly Precipation

3. The table shows the results of a survey that asked high school students how many hours a week they listen to music.

   a. Make a double box-and-whisker plot that represents the data. Describe the shape of each distribution.

	Females	Males
Survey size	50	58
Minimum	16	18
Maximum	40	52
1st Quartile	24	30
Median	28	38
3rd Quartile	32	46
Mean	28	30
Standard deviation	6	12

   b. Compare the number of hours of music listened to by females to the number of hours of music listened to by males.

   c. About how many females surveyed would you expect to listen to music between 22 and 34 hours per week?

   d. If you survey 100 more females, about how many would you expect to listen to music between 16 and 40 hours per week?

Name_____ Date_____

Essential Question How can you read and make a two-way table?

1 **EXPLORATION:** Reading a Two-Way Table

Work with a partner. You are the manager of a sports shop. The two-way tables show the numbers of soccer T-shirts in stock at your shop at the beginning and end of the selling season. (a) Complete the totals for the rows and columns in each table. (b) How would you alter the number of T-shirts you order for next season? Explain your reasoning.

Beginning of season		T-Shirt Size					
		S	M	L	XL	XXL	Total
Color	blue/white	5	6	7	6	5	
	blue/gold	5	6	7	6	5	
	red/white	5	6	7	6	5	
	black/white	5	6	7	6	5	
	black/gold	5	6	7	6	5	
	Total						145

End of season		T-Shirt Size					
		S	M	L	XL	XXL	Total
Color	blue/white	5	4	1	0	2	
	blue/gold	3	6	5	2	0	
	red/white	4	2	4	1	3	
	black/white	3	4	1	2	1	
	black/gold	5	2	3	0	2	
	Total						

7.4 Two-Way Tables (continued)

2 EXPLORATION: Making a Two-Way Table

Work with a partner. The three-dimensional bar graph shows the numbers of hours students work at part-time jobs.

a. Make a two-way table showing the data. Use estimation to find the entries in your table.

Part-Time Jobs of Students at a High School

b. Write two observations that summarize the data in your table.

Communicate Your Answer

3. How can you read and make a two-way table?

7.4 Notetaking with Vocabulary
For use after Lesson 7.4

In your own words, write the meaning of each vocabulary term.

two-way table

joint frequency

marginal frequency

joint relative frequency

marginal relative frequency

conditional relative frequency

Core Concepts

Relative Frequencies

A **joint relative frequency** is the ratio of a frequency that is not in the "total" row or the "total" column to the total number of values or observations.

A **marginal relative frequency** is the sum of the joint relative frequencies in a row or column.

When finding relative frequencies in a two-way table, you can use the corresponding decimals or percents.

Notes:

Name _____ Date _____

Conditional Relative Frequencies

A **conditional relative frequency** is the ratio of a joint relative frequency to the marginal relative frequency. You can find a conditional relative frequency using a row total or a column total of a two-way table.

Notes:

Extra Practice

In Exercises 1 and 2, find and interpret the marginal frequencies.

1.

		Attend College	
		Yes	No
Gender	Male	98	132
	Female	120	88

2.

		Own a Car	
		Yes	No
Gender	Male	54	136
	Female	45	137

3. You conduct a survey that asks 85 students in your school whether they are in Math Club or Chess Club. Thirty-five of the students are in Math Club, and 20 of those students are also in Chess Club. Thirty-eight of the students are not in Math Club or Chess Club. Organize the results in a two-way table. Include the marginal frequencies.

7.4 Notetaking with Vocabulary (continued)

4. Make a two-way table that shows the joint and marginal relative frequencies.

<table>
<tr><th></th><th></th><th colspan="2">Read Catcher in the Rye</th></tr>
<tr><th></th><th></th><th>Yes</th><th>No</th></tr>
<tr><th rowspan="2">Gender</th><th>Male</th><td>96</td><td>80</td></tr>
<tr><th>Female</th><td>54</td><td>88</td></tr>
</table>

5. A company is organizing a baseball game for their employees. The employees are asked whether they prefer to attend a day game or a night game. They are also asked whether they prefer to sit in the upper deck or lower deck. The results are shown in a two-way table. Make a two-way table that shows the conditional relative frequencies based on the row totals. Given that an employee prefers to go to a day game, what is the conditional relative frequency that he or she prefers to sit in the lower deck?

<table>
<tr><th></th><th></th><th colspan="2">Seat</th></tr>
<tr><th></th><th></th><th>Upper</th><th>Lower</th></tr>
<tr><th rowspan="2">Game Time</th><th>Day</th><td>28</td><td>34</td></tr>
<tr><th>Night</th><td>22</td><td>52</td></tr>
</table>

7.5 Choosing a Data Display
For use with Exploration 7.5

Essential Question How can you display data in a way that helps you make decisions?

---

1 EXPLORATION: Displaying Data

Work with a partner. Analyze the data and then create a display that best represents the data. Explain your choice of data display.

a. A group of schools in New England participated in a 2-month study and reported 3962 animals found dead along roads.

  birds: 307

  mammals: 2746

  amphibians: 145

  reptiles: 75

  unknown: 689

b. The data below show the numbers of black bears killed on a state's roads from 1993 to 2012.

1993: 30	2003: 74
1994: 37	2004: 88
1995: 46	2005: 82
1996: 33	2006: 109
1997: 43	2007: 99
1998: 35	2008: 129
1999: 43	2009: 111
2000: 47	2010: 127
2001: 49	2011: 141
2002: 61	2012: 135

c. A 1-week study along a 4-mile section of road found the following weights (in pounds) of raccoons that had been killed by vehicles.

13.4	14.8	17.0	12.9	21.3	21.5	16.8	14.8
15.2	18.7	18.6	17.2	18.5	9.4	19.4	15.7
14.5	9.5	25.4	21.5	17.3	19.1	11.0	12.4
20.4	13.6	17.5	18.5	21.5	14.0	13.9	19.0

7.5 Choosing a Data Display (continued)

1 EXPLORATION: Displaying Data (continued)

d. A yearlong study by volunteers in California reported the following numbers of animals killed by motor vehicles.

raccoons: 1693   gray squirrels: 715

skunks: 1372   cottontail rabbits: 629

ground squirrels: 845   barn owls: 486

opossum: 763   jackrabbits: 466

deer: 761   gopher snakes: 363

Communicate Your Answer

2. How can you display data in a way that helps you make decisions?

3. Use the Internet or some other reference to find examples of the following types of data displays.

bar graph   circle graph   scatter plot

stem-and-leaf plot   pictograph   line graph

box-and-whisker plot   histogram   dot plot

7.5 Notetaking with Vocabulary
For use after Lesson 7.5

In your own words, write the meaning of each vocabulary term.

qualitative (categorical) data

quantitative data

misleading graph

Core Concepts

Types of Data

Qualitative data, or **categorical data,** consist of labels or nonnumerical entries that can be separated into different categories. When using qualitative data, operations such as adding or finding a mean do not make sense.

Quantitative data consist of numbers that represent counts or measurements.

Notes:

7.5 Notetaking with Vocabulary (continued)

Extra Practice

In Exercises 1–4, tell whether the data are *qualitative* or *quantitative*. Explain your reasoning.

1. bookmarks in your web browser

2. heights of players on a basketball team

3. the number of kilobytes in a downloaded file

4. FM radio station numbers

In Exercises 5 and 6, analyze the data and then create a display that best represents the data. Explain your reasoning.

5.

Home Runs Each Year											
Babe Ruth						**Hank Aaron**					
0	4	3	2	11	29	13	27	26	44	30	39
54	59	35	41	46	25	40	34	45	44	24	32
47	60	54	46	49	46	44	39	29	44	38	47
41	34	22	6			34	40	20	12	10	

7.5 Notetaking with Vocabulary (continued)

6.

Total Points Scored by a Basketball Team for Each Game					
48	56	49	52	40	65
30	47	62	40	59	37
45	41	44	33	44	30

In Exercises 7 and 8, describe how the graph is misleading. Then explain how someone might misinterpret the graph.

7.

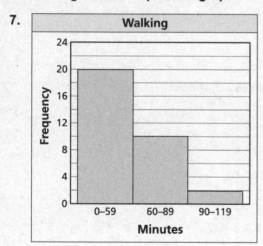

8.

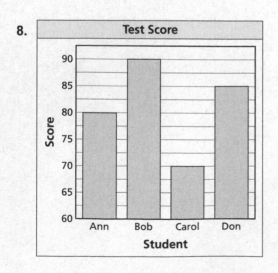

Chapter 8 Maintaining Mathematical Proficiency

Simplify the expression.

1. $\left| -3 + (-1) \right| =$

2. $\left| 10 - 11 \right| =$

3. $\left| -6 + 8 \right| =$

4. $\left| 9 - (-1) \right| =$

5. $\left| -12 - (-8) \right| =$

6. $\left| -15 - 7 \right| =$

7. $\left| -12 + 3 \right| =$

8. $\left| 5 + (-15) \right| =$

9. $\left| 1 - 12 \right| =$

Find the area of the triangle.

10.

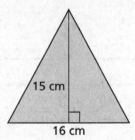

15 cm

16 cm

11.

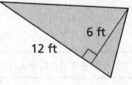

6 ft

12 ft

12.

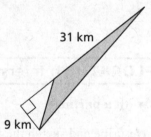

31 km

9 km

8.1 Points, Lines, and Planes
For use with Exploration 8.1

Essential Question How can you use dynamic geometry software to visualize geometric concepts?

1 EXPLORATION: Using Dynamic Geometry Software

Go to *BigIdeasMath.com* for an interactive tool to investigate this exploration.

Work with a partner. Use dynamic geometry software to draw several points. Also, draw some lines, line segments, and rays. What is the difference between a line, a line segment, and a ray?

Sample

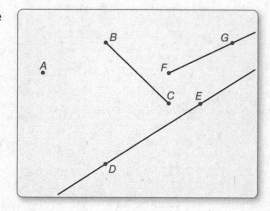

2 EXPLORATION: Intersections of Lines and Planes

Work with a partner.

a. Describe and sketch the ways in which two lines can intersect or not intersect. Give examples of each using the lines formed by the walls, floor, and ceiling in your classroom.

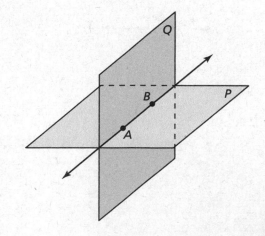

8.1 **Points, Lines, and Planes** (continued)

2 **EXPLORATION: Intersections of Lines and Planes** (continued)

b. Describe and sketch the ways in which a line and a plane can intersect or not intersect. Give examples of each using the walls, floor, and ceiling in your classroom.

c. Describe and sketch the ways in which two planes can intersect or not intersect. Give examples of each using the walls, floor, and ceiling in your classroom.

3 **EXPLORATION: Exploring Dynamic Geometry Software**

Go to *BigIdeasMath.com* for an interactive tool to investigate this exploration.

Work with a partner. Use dynamic geometry software to explore geometry. Use the software to find a term or concept that is unfamiliar to you. Then use the capabilities of the software to determine the meaning of the term or concept.

Communicate Your Answer

4. How can you use dynamic geometry software to visualize geometric concepts?

8.1 Notetaking with Vocabulary
For use after Lesson 8.1

In your own words, write the meaning of each vocabulary term.

undefined terms

point

line

plane

collinear points

coplanar points

defined terms

line segment, or segment

endpoints

ray

opposite rays

intersection

8.1 **Notetaking with Vocabulary** (continued)

Core Concepts

Undefined Terms: Point, Line, and Plane

Point A **point** has no dimension.
A dot represents a point.

$\overset{\textstyle A}{\bullet}$

point A

Line A **line** has one dimension. It is represented by a line with two arrowheads, but it extends without end.

Through any two points, there is exactly one line. You can use any two points on a line to name it.

line ℓ, line AB ($\overleftrightarrow{AB}$), or line BA ($\overleftrightarrow{BA}$)

Plane A **plane** has two dimensions. It is represented by a shape that looks like a floor or a wall, but it extends without end.

Through any three points not on the same line, there is exactly one plane. You can use three points that are not all on the same line to name a plane.

plane M, or plane ABC

Notes:

Defined Terms: Segment and Ray

The definitions below use line AB $\left(\text{written as } \overleftrightarrow{AB}\right)$ and points A and B.

line

Segment The **line segment** AB, or **segment** AB $\left(\text{written as } \overline{AB}\right)$ consists of the **endpoints** A and B and all points on $\overleftrightarrow{AB}$ that are between A and B. Note that $\overline{AB}$ can also be named $\overline{BA}$.

segment

endpoint   endpoint
A   B

Ray The **ray** AB $\left(\text{written as } \overrightarrow{AB}\right)$ consists of the endpoint A and all points on $\overleftrightarrow{AB}$ that lie on the same side of A as B.

Note that $\overrightarrow{AB}$ and $\overrightarrow{BA}$ are different rays.

ray

endpoint
A   B

endpoint
A   B

Opposite Rays If point C lies on $\overleftrightarrow{AB}$ between A and B, then $\overrightarrow{CA}$ and $\overrightarrow{CB}$ are **opposite rays**.

A   C   B

Notes:

8.1 **Notetaking with Vocabulary (continued)**

Extra Practice

In Exercises 1–4, use the diagram.

1. Give two other names for $\overleftrightarrow{CD}$.

2. Give another name for plane M.

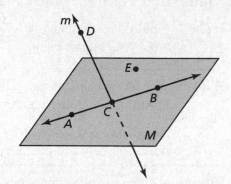

3. Name three points that are collinear. Then name a fourth point that is not collinear with these three points.

4. Name a point that is not coplanar with points A, C, E.

In Exercises 5–8, use the diagram.

5. What is another name for $\overrightarrow{PQ}$?

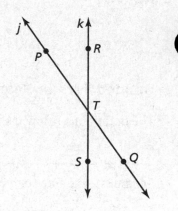

6. What is another name for $\overleftrightarrow{RS}$?

7. Name all rays with endpoint T. Which of these rays are opposite rays?

8. On the diagram, draw planes M and N that intersect at line k.

In Exercises 9 and 10, sketch the figure described.

9. $\overline{AB}$ and $\overrightarrow{BC}$

10. line k in plane M

8.2 Measuring and Constructing Segments
For use with Exploration 8.2

Essential Question How can you measure and construct a line segment?

EXPLORATION: Measuring Line Segments Using Nonstandard Units

Work with a partner.

a. Draw a line segment that has a length of 6 inches.

b. Use a standard-sized paper clip to measure the length of the line segment. Explain how you measured the line segment in "paper clips."

c. Write conversion factors from paper clips to inches and vice versa.

1 paper clip = ____ in.

1 in. = ____ paper clip

d. A *straightedge* is a tool that you can use to draw a straight line. An example of a straightedge is a ruler. Use only a pencil, straightedge, paper clip, and paper to draw another line segment that is 6 inches long. Explain your process.

8.2 **Measuring and Constructing Segments** (continued)

2 **EXPLORATION:** Measuring Line Segments Using Nonstandard Units

Work with a partner.

   a. Fold a 3-inch by 5-inch index card on one of its diagonals.

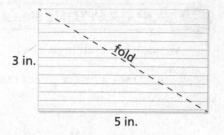

   b. Use the Pythagorean Theorem to algebraically determine the length of the diagonal in inches. Use a ruler to check your answer.

   c. Measure the length and width of the index card in paper clips.

   d. Use the Pythagorean Theorem to algebraically determine the length of the diagonal in paper clips. Then check your answer by measuring the length of the diagonal in paper clips. Does the Pythagorean Theorem work for any unit of measure? Justify your answer.

3 **EXPLORATION:** Measuring Heights Using Nonstandard Units

Work with a partner. Consider a unit of length that is equal to the length of the diagonal you found in Exploration 2. Call this length "1 diag." How tall are you in diags? Explain how you obtained your answer.

Communicate Your Answer

   4. How can you measure and construct a line segment?

Name_____ Date_____

8.2 Notetaking with Vocabulary
For use after Lesson 8.2

In your own words, write the meaning of each vocabulary term.

postulate

axiom

coordinate

distance

construction

congruent segments

between

Ruler Postulate

The points on a line can be matched one to one with the real numbers. The real number that corresponds to a point is the **coordinate** of the point.

The **distance** between points A and B, written as AB, is the absolute value of the difference of the coordinates of A and B.

Notes:

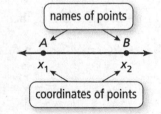

$$AB = |x_2 - x_1|$$

8.2 Notetaking with Vocabulary (continued)

Core Concepts

Congruent Segments

Line segments that have the same length are called **congruent segments**. You can say
"the length of $\overline{AB}$ is equal to the length of $\overline{CD}$," or you can say "$\overline{AB}$ *is congruent to*
$\overline{CD}$." The symbol $\cong$ means "is congruent to."

Lengths are equal.	**Segments are congruent.**
$AB = CD$	$\overline{AB} \cong \overline{CD}$
"is equal to"	"is congruent to"

Notes:

Segment Addition Postulate

If B is between A and C, then $AB + BC = AC$.

If $AB + BC = AC$, then B is between A and C.

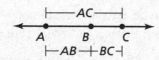

Notes:

Name_____ Date_____

Extra Practice

In Exercises 1–3, plot the points in the coordinate plane. Then determine whether $\overline{AB}$ and $\overline{CD}$ are congruent.

1. $A(-5, 5)$, $B(-2, 5)$
   $C(2, -4)$, $D(-1, -4)$

2. $A(4, 0)$, $B(4, 3)$
   $C(-4, -4)$, $D(-4, 1)$

3. $A(-1, 5)$, $B(5, 5)$
   $C(1, 3)$, $D(1, -3)$

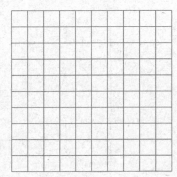
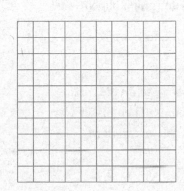
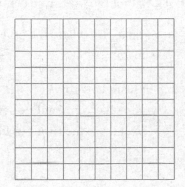

In Exercises 4–6, find **VW**.

4.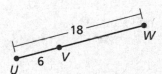

5.

6.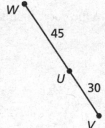

7. A bookstore and a movie theater are 6 kilometers apart along the same street. A florist is located between the bookstore and the theater on the same street. The florist is 2.5 kilometers from the theater. How far is the florist from the bookstore?

8.3 Using Midpoint and Distance Formulas

For use with Exploration 8.3

Essential Question How can you find the midpoint and length of a line segment in a coordinate plane?

---

1 **EXPLORATION:** Finding the Midpoint of a Line Segment

> **Work with a partner.** Use centimeter graph paper.

a. Graph $\overline{AB}$, where the points A and B are as shown.

b. Explain how to *bisect* $\overline{AB}$, that is, to divide $\overline{AB}$ into two congruent line segments. Then bisect $\overline{AB}$ and use the result to find the *midpoint M* of $\overline{AB}$.

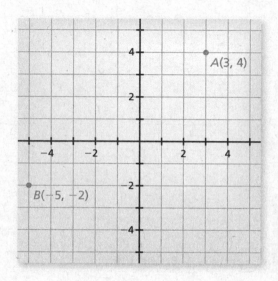

c. What are the coordinates of the midpoint M?

d. Compare the x-coordinates of A, B, and M. Compare the y-coordinates of A, B, and M. How are the coordinates of the midpoint M related to the coordinates of A and B?

8.3   **Using Midpoint and Distance Formulas** (continued)

---

2   **EXPLORATION:** Finding the Length of a Line Segment

Work with a partner. Use centimeter graph paper.

a. Add point *C* to your graph as shown.

b. Use the Pythagorean Theorem to find the length of $\overline{AB}$.

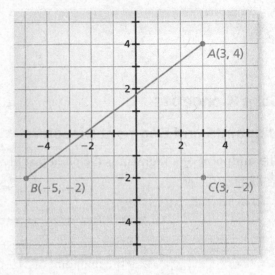

c. Use a centimeter ruler to verify the length you found in part (b).

d. Use the Pythagorean Theorem and point *M* from Exploration 1 to find the lengths of $\overline{AM}$ and $\overline{MB}$. What can you conclude?

Communicate Your Answer

3. How can you find the midpoint and length of a line segment in a coordinate plane?

4. Find the coordinates of the midpoint *M* and the length of the line segment whose endpoints are given.

   a. $D(-10, -4)$, $E(14, 6)$ b. $F(-4, 8)$, $G(9, 0)$

8.3 Notetaking with Vocabulary
For use after Lesson 8.3

In your own words, write the meaning of each vocabulary term.

midpoint

segment bisector

Core Concepts

Midpoints and Segment Bisectors

The **midpoint** of a segment is the point that divides the segment into two congruent segments.

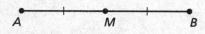

M is the midpoint of $\overline{AB}$.
So, $\overline{AM} \cong \overline{MB}$ and $AM = MB$.

A **segment bisector** is a point, ray, line, line segment, or plane that intersects the segment at its midpoint. A midpoint or a segment bisector *bisects* a segment.

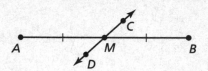

$\overleftrightarrow{CD}$ is a segment bisector of $\overline{AB}$.
So, $\overline{AM} \cong \overline{MB}$ and $AM = MB$.

Notes:

8.3 **Notetaking with Vocabulary** (continued)

The Midpoint Formula

The coordinates of the midpoint of a segment are the averages of the x-coordinates and of the y-coordinates of the endpoints.

If $A(x_1, y_1)$ and $B(x_2, y_2)$ are points in a coordinate plane, then the midpoint M of $\overline{AB}$ has coordinates

$$\left(\frac{x_1 + x_2}{2}, \frac{y_1 + y_2}{2}\right).$$

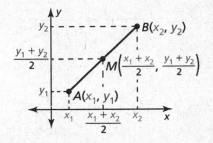

Notes:

The Distance Formula

If $A(x_1, y_1)$ and $B(x_2, y_2)$ are points in a coordinate plane, then the distance between A and B is

$$AB = \sqrt{(x_2 - x_1)^2 + (y_2 - y_1)^2}.$$

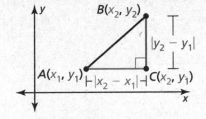

Notes:

8.3 **Notetaking with Vocabulary** (continued)

Extra Practice

In Exercises 1–3, identify the segment bisector of $\overline{AB}$. Then find AB.

1.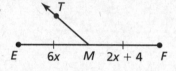

2.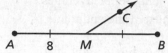

3.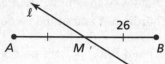

In Exercises 4-6, identify the segment bisector of $\overline{EF}$. Then find EF.

4.   **5.**   **6.**

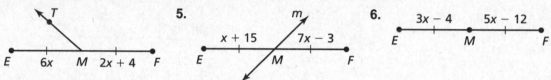

In Exercises 7–9, the endpoints of $\overline{PQ}$ are given. Find the coordinates of the midpoint M.

7. $P(-4, 3)$ and $Q(0, 5)$ **8.** $P(-2, 7)$ and $Q(10, -3)$ **9.** $P(3, -15)$ and $Q(9, -3)$

In Exercises 10–12, the midpoint M and one endpoint of $\overline{JK}$ are given. Find the coordinates of the other endpoint.

10. $J(7, 2)$ and $M(1, -2)$ **11.** $J(5, -2)$ and $M(0, -1)$ **12.** $J(2, 16)$ and $M\left(-\frac{9}{2}, 7\right)$

8.4 Perimeter and Area in the Coordinate Plane
For use with Exploration 8.4

Essential Question How can you find the perimeter and area of a polygon in a coordinate plane?

1 EXPLORATION: Finding the Perimeter and Area of a Quadrilateral

Work with a partner.

a. On the centimeter graph paper, draw quadrilateral $ABCD$ in a coordinate plane. Label the points $A(1, 4)$, $B(-3, 1)$, $C(0, -3)$, and $D(4, 0)$.

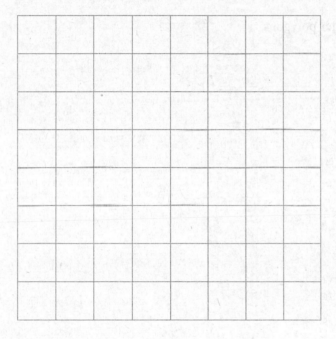

b. Find the perimeter of quadrilateral $ABCD$.

c. Are adjacent sides of quadrilateral $ABCD$ perpendicular to each other? How can you tell?

d. What is the definition of a square? Is quadrilateral $ABCD$ a square? Justify your answer. Find the area of quadrilateral $ABCD$.

Name _____ Date _____

2 **EXPLORATION: Finding the Area of a Polygon**

Work with a partner.

a. Quadrilateral *ABCD* is partitioned into four right triangles and one square, as shown. Find the coordinates of the vertices for the five smaller polygons.

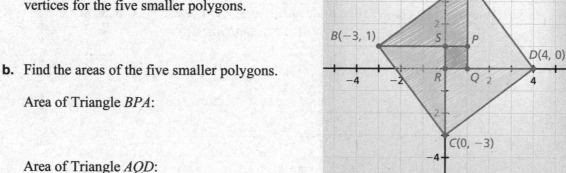

b. Find the areas of the five smaller polygons.

Area of Triangle *BPA*:

Area of Triangle *AQD*:

Area of Triangle *DRC*:

Area of Triangle *CSB*:

Area of Square *PQRS*:

c. Is the sum of the areas of the five smaller polygons equal to the area of quadrilateral *ABCD*? Justify your answer.

Communicate Your Answer

3. How can you find the perimeter and area of a polygon in a coordinate plane?

4. Repeat Exploration 1 for quadrilateral *EFGH*, where the coordinates of the vertices are *E*(−3, 6), *F*(−7, 3), *G*(−1, −5), and *H*(3, −2).

8.4

Notetaking with Vocabulary
For use after Lesson 8.4

In your own words, write the meaning of each vocabulary term.

inscribed circle

circumscribed circle

polygon

side

vertex

n-gon

convex

concave

regular polygon

Core Concepts

Polygons

In geometry, a figure that lies in a plane is called a plane figure. Recall that a *polygon* is a closed plane figure formed by three or more line segments called *sides*. Each side intersects exactly two sides, one at each *vertex*, so that no two sides with a common vertex are collinear. You can name a polygon by listing the vertices in consecutive order.

side $\overline{BC}$ vertex *D*

polygon *ABCDE*

Notes:

Integrated Mathematics I   **233**
Student Journal

8.4 Notetaking with Vocabulary (continued)

Inscribed Polygon

A polygon is an **inscribed polygon** when all its vertices lie on a circle. The circle that contains the vertices is a **circumscribed circle**.

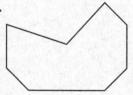

Notes:

Extra Practice

In Exercises 1–4, classify the polygon by the number of sides. Tell whether it is *convex* **or** *concave*.

1.

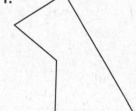

2.

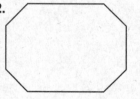

3.

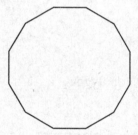

4.

In Exercises 5–8, find the perimeter and area of the polygon with the given vertices.

5. $X(2, 4)$, $Y(0, -2)$, $Z(2, -2)$

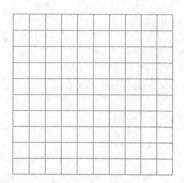

6. $P(1, 3)$, $Q(1, 1)$, $R(-4, 2)$

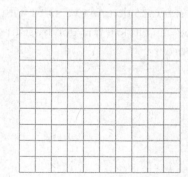

8.4 **Notetaking with Vocabulary** (continued)

7. $J(-4, 1), K(-4, -2), L(6, -2), M(6, 1)$ 8. $D(5, -3), E(5, -6), F(2, -6), G(2, -3)$

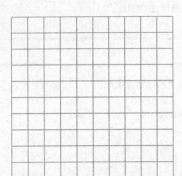   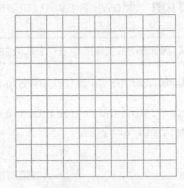

In Exercises 9–14, use the diagram.

9. Find the perimeter of $\triangle ABD$.

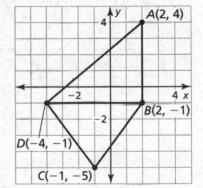

10. Find the perimeter of $\triangle BCD$.

11. Find the perimeter of quadrilateral $ABCD$.

12. Find the area of $\triangle ABD$.

13. Find the area of $\triangle BCD$.

14. Find the area of quadrilateral $ABCD$.

Name_____ Date _____

Essential Question How can you measure and classify an angle?

---

1 **EXPLORATION:** Measuring and Classifying Angles

Go to *BigIdeasMath.com* for an interactive tool to investigate this exploration.

Work with a partner. Find the degree measure of each of the following angles. Classify each angle as acute, right, or obtuse.

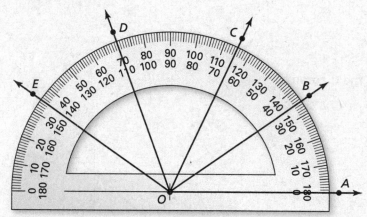

   a. ∠AOB

   b. ∠AOC

   c. ∠BOC

   d. ∠BOE

   e. ∠COE

   f. ∠COD

   g. ∠BOD

   h. ∠AOE

8.5 **Measuring and Constructing Angles** (continued)

---

2 **EXPLORATION:** Drawing a Regular Polygon

Go to *BigIdeasMath.com* for an interactive tool to investigate this exploration.

Work with a partner.

a. On a separate sheet of paper or an index card, use a ruler and protractor to draw the triangular pattern shown at the right.

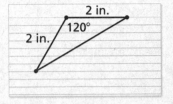

b. Cut out the pattern and use it to draw three regular hexagons, as shown in your book.

c. The sum of the angle measures of a polygon with n sides is equal to $180(n - 2)°$.

Do the angle measures of your hexagons agree with this rule? Explain.

d. Partition your hexagons into smaller polygons, as shown in your book. For each hexagon, find the sum of the angle measures of the smaller polygons. Does each sum equal the sum of the angle measures of a hexagon? Explain.

Communicate Your Answer

3. How can you measure and classify an angle?

Name ______________________________ Date __________

8.5 Notetaking with Vocabulary

For use after Lesson 8.5

In your own words, write the meaning of each vocabulary term.

angle

vertex

sides of an angle

interior of an angle

exterior of an angle

measure of an angle

acute angle

right angle

obtuse angle

straight angle

congruent angles

angle bisector

8.5   **Notetaking with Vocabulary** (continued)

Protractor Postulate

Consider $\overrightarrow{OB}$ and a point A on one side of $\overrightarrow{OB}$. The rays of the form $\overrightarrow{OA}$ can be matched one to one with the real numbers from 0 to 180.

The **measure** of $\angle AOB$, which can be written as $m\angle AOB$, is equal to the absolute value of the difference between the real numbers matched with $\overrightarrow{OA}$ and $\overrightarrow{OB}$ on a protractor.

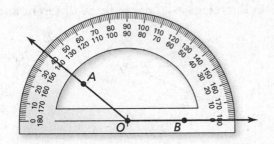

Notes:

Core Concepts

Types of Angles

  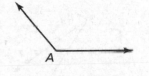

    acute angle   **right angle**   **obtuse angle**   **straight angle**

Measures greater than   Measures 90°   Measures greater than   Measures 180°
0° and less than 90°   90° and less than 180°

Notes:

Angle Addition Postulate

Words   If P is the interior of $\angle RST$, then the measure of
          $\angle RST$ is equal to the sum of the measures of
          $\angle RSP$ and $\angle PST$.

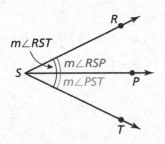

Symbols   If P is in the interior of $\angle RST$, then
            $m\angle RST = m\angle RSP + m\angle PST$.

Notes:

8.5 **Notetaking with Vocabulary** (continued)

Extra Practice

In Exercises 1–3, name three different angles in the diagram.

1.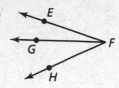

2.

3.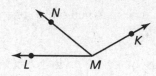

In Exercises 4–9, find the indicated angle measure(s).

4. Find $m\angle JKL$.

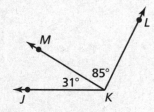

5. $m\angle RSU = 91°$.
Find $m\angle RST$.

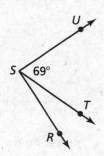

6. $\angle UWX$ is a straight angle.
Find $m\angle UWV$ and $m\angle XWV$.

U   W   X
$(x + 20)°$ $x°$
V

7. Find $m\angle CAD$
and $m\angle BAD$.

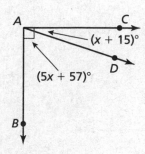

8. $\overrightarrow{EG}$ bisects $\angle DEF$.
Find $m\angle DEG$ and
$m\angle GEF$.

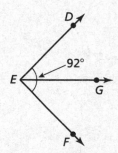

9. $\overrightarrow{QR}$ bisects $\angle PQS$.
Find $m\angle PQR$ and
$m\angle PQS$.

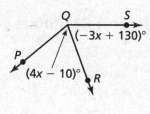

8.6 Describing Pairs of Angles
For use with Exploration 8.6

Essential Question How can you describe angle pair relationships and use these descriptions to find angle measures?

---

1 EXPLORATION: Finding Angle Measures

Work with a partner. The five-pointed star has a regular pentagon at its center.

a. What do you notice about the following angle pairs?

$x°$ and $y°$

$y°$ and $z°$

$x°$ and $z°$

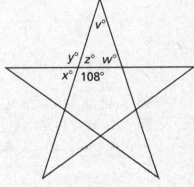

b. Find the values of the indicated variables. Do not use a protractor to measure the angles.

$x =$

$y =$

$z =$

$w =$

$v =$

Explain how you obtained each answer.

8.6 **Describing Pairs of Angles** (continued)

---

2 **EXPLORATION:** Finding Angle Measures

Work with a partner. A square is divided by its diagonals into four triangles.

a. What do you notice about the following angle pairs?

$a°$ and $b°$

$c°$ and $d°$

$c°$ and $e°$

b. Find the values of the indicated variables. Do not use a protractor to measure the angles.

$c =$

$d =$

$e =$

Explain how you obtained each answer.

Communicate Your Answer

3. How can you describe angle pair relationships and use these descriptions to find angle measures?

4. What do you notice about the angle measures of complementary angles, supplementary angles, and vertical angles?

8.6 Notetaking with Vocabulary
For use after Lesson 8.6

In your own words, write the meaning of each vocabulary term.

complementary angles

supplementary angles

adjacent angles

linear pair

vertical angles

Core Concepts

Complementary and Supplementary Angles

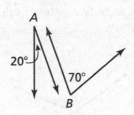

∠1 and ∠2   ∠A and ∠B

complementary angles

Two positive angles whose measures have a sum of 90°. Each angle is the *complement* of the other.

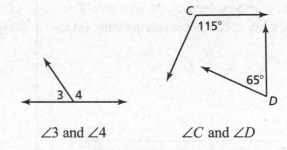

∠3 and ∠4   ∠C and ∠D

supplementary angles

Two positive angles whose measures have a sum of 180°. Each angle is the *supplement* of the other.

Notes:

8.6 **Notetaking with Vocabulary** (continued)

Adjacent Angles

Complementary angles and supplementary angles can be *adjacent angles* or *nonadjacent angles*. **Adjacent angles** are two angles that share a common vertex and side, but have no common interior points.

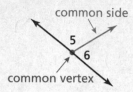

common side

5
6

common vertex

∠5 and ∠6 are adjacent angles

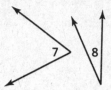

7   8

∠7 and ∠8 are nonadjacent angles.

Notes:

Linear Pairs and Vertical Angles

Two adjacent angles are a **linear pair** when their noncommon sides are opposite rays. The angles in a linear pair are supplementary angles.

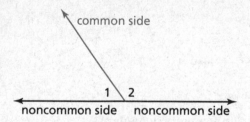

common side

1   2

noncommon side   noncommon side

∠1 and ∠2 are a linear pair.

Two angles are **vertical angles** when their sides form two pairs of opposite rays.

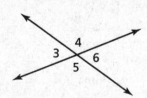

4
3   6
5

∠3 and ∠6 are vertical angles.

∠4 and ∠5 are vertical angles.

Notes:

8.6 **Notetaking with Vocabulary** (continued)

Extra Practice

In Exercises 1 and 2, use the figure.

1. Name the pair(s) of adjacent complementary angles.

2. Name the pair(s) of nonadjacent supplementary angles.

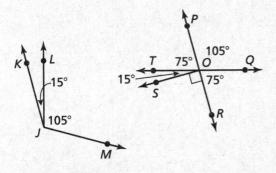

In Exercises 3 and 4, find the angle measure.

3. $\angle A$ is a complement of $\angle B$ and $m\angle A = 36°$. Find $m\angle B$.

4. $\angle C$ is a supplement of $\angle D$ and $m\angle D = 117°$. Find $m\angle C$.

In Exercises 5 and 6, find the measure of each angle.

5.

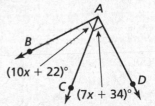

6.

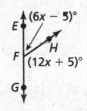

In Exercises 7–9, use the figure.

7. Identify the linear pair(s) that include $\angle 1$.

8. Identify the vertical angles.

9. Are $\angle 6$ and $\angle 7$ a linear pair? Explain.

Chapter 9 Maintaining Mathematical Proficiency

Write an equation for the *n*th term of the arithmetic sequence. Then find a_{20}.

1. 5, 11, 17, 23, …

2. 22, 34, 46, 58, …

3. −13, 0, 13, 26, …

4. −4.5, −4.0, −3.5, −3.0, …

5. 40, 25, 10, −5, …

6. $-\frac{1}{2}, \frac{1}{2}, \frac{3}{2}, \frac{5}{2}, \ldots$

Solve the equation.

7. $3x - 9 = 12$

8. $16 - 4y = 40$

9. $6z + 5 = 23$

10. $15 = 11q - 18$

11. $6r + 3 = 33$

12. $27 = 4s - 9$

9.1 Conditional Statements
For use with Exploration 9.1

Essential Question   When is a conditional statement true or false?

A *conditional statement*, symbolized by $p \rightarrow q$, can be written as an "if-then statement" in which p is the *hypothesis* and q is the *conclusion*. Here is an example.

If a polygon is a triangle, then the sum of its angle measures is 180°.

    hypothesis, p conclusion, q

1   EXPLORATION: Determining Whether a Statement Is True or False

Work with a partner. A hypothesis can either be true or false. The same is true of a conclusion. For a conditional statement to be true, the hypothesis and conclusion do not necessarily both have to be true. Determine whether each conditional statement is true or false. Justify your answer.

  a. If yesterday was Wednesday, then today is Thursday.

  b. If an angle is acute, then it has a measure of 30°.

  c. If a month has 30 days, then it is June.

  d. If an even number is not divisible by 2, then 9 is a perfect cube.

2   EXPLORATION: Determining Whether a Statement Is True or False?

Work with a partner. Use the points in the coordinate plane to determine whether each statement is true or false. Justify your answer.

  a. $\triangle ABC$ is a right triangle.

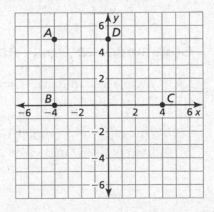

9.1 **Conditional Statements** (continued)

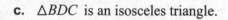

2 **EXPLORATION:** Determining Whether a Statement Is True or False (continued)

b. △*BDC* is an equilateral triangle.

c. △*BDC* is an isosceles triangle.

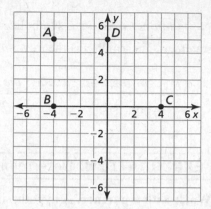

d. Quadrilateral *ABCD* is a trapezoid.

e. Quadrilateral *ABCD* is a parallelogram.

3 **EXPLORATION:** Determining Whether a Statement Is True or False

Work with a partner. Determine whether each conditional statement is true or false. Justify your answer.

a. If △*ADC* is a right triangle, then the Pythagorean Theorem is valid for △*ADC*.

b. If ∠*A* and ∠*B* are complementary, then the sum of their measures is 180°.

c. If figure *ABCD* is a quadrilateral, then the sum of its angle measures is 180°.

d. If points *A*, *B*, and *C* are collinear, then they lie on the same line.

e. If $\overleftrightarrow{AB}$ and $\overleftrightarrow{BD}$ intersect at a point, then they form two pairs of vertical angles.

Communicate Your Answer

4. When is a conditional statement true or false?

5. Write one true conditional statement and one false conditional statement that are different from those given in Exploration 3. Justify your answer.

Name_____ Date_____

9.1 Notetaking with Vocabulary
For use after Lesson 9.1

In your own words, write the meaning of each vocabulary term.

conditional statement

if-then form

hypothesis

conclusion

negation

converse

inverse

contrapositive

equivalent statements

perpendicular lines

biconditional statement

truth value

truth table

9.1 Notetaking with Vocabulary (continued)

Core Concepts

Conditional Statement

A **conditional statement** is a logical statement that has two parts, a *hypothesis p* and a *conclusion q*. When a conditional statement is written in **if-then form**, the "if" part contains the **hypothesis** and the "then" part contains the **conclusion**.

Words   If p, then q.   **Symbols** $p \rightarrow q$ (read as "p implies q")

Notes:

Negation

The **negation** of a statement is the *opposite* of the original statement. To write the negation of a statement p, you write the symbol for negation ($\sim$) before the letter. So, "not p" is written $\sim p$.

Words   not p **Symbols** $\sim p$

Notes:

Related Conditionals

Consider the conditional statement below.

Words	If p, then q.	**Symbols**	$p \rightarrow q$

Converse	To write the **converse** of a conditional statement, exchange the hypothesis and the conclusion.		

Words	If q, then p.	**Symbols**	$q \rightarrow p$

Inverse	To write the **inverse** of a conditional statement, negate both the hypothesis and the conclusion.		

Words	If not p, then not q.	**Symbols**	$\sim p \rightarrow \sim q$

9.1 **Notetaking with Vocabulary** (continued)

Related Conditionals (continued)

Contrapositive To write the **contrapositive** of a conditional statement, first write the converse. Then negate both the hypothesis and the conclusion.

Words   If not q, then not p.   **Symbols** $\sim q \rightarrow \sim p$

A conditional statement and its contrapositive are either both true or both false. Similarly, the converse and inverse of a conditional statement are either both true or both false. In general, when two statements are both true or both false, they are called **equivalent statements**.

Notes:

Biconditional Statement

When a conditional statement and its converse are both true, you can write them as a single *biconditional statement*. A **biconditional statement** is a statement that contains the phrase "if and only if."

Words p if and only if q **Symbols** $p \leftrightarrow q$

Any definition can be written as a biconditional statement.

Notes:

9.1 Notetaking with Vocabulary (continued)

Extra Practice

In Exercises 1 and 2, rewrite the conditional statement in if-then form.

1. $13x - 5 = -18$, because $x = -1$.

2. The sum of the measures of interior angles of a triangle is $180°$.

3. Let p be "Quadrilateral $ABCD$ is a rectangle" and let q be "the sum of the angle measures is $360°$." Write the conditional statement $p \rightarrow q$, the converse $q \rightarrow p$, the inverse $\sim p \rightarrow \sim q$, and the contrapositive $\sim q \rightarrow \sim p$ in words. Then decide whether each statement is true or false.

In Exercises 4–6, decide whether the statement about the diagram is true. Explain your answer using the definitions you have learned.

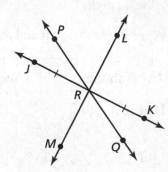

4. $\overline{LM}$ bisects $\overline{JK}$

5. $\angle JRP$ and $\angle PRL$ are complementary.

6. $\angle MRQ \cong \angle PRL$

Name_____ Date_____

9.2 Inductive and Deductive Reasoning
For use with Exploration 9.2

Essential Question How can you use reasoning to solve problems?

Recall that conjecture is an unproven statement about a general mathematical concept that is based on observations.

1 EXPLORATION: Writing a Conjecture

Work with a partner. Write a conjecture about the pattern. Then use your conjecture to draw the 10th object in the pattern.

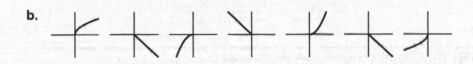

2 EXPLORATION: Using a Venn Diagram

Work with a partner. Use the Venn diagram to determine whether the statement is true or false. Justify your answer. Assume that no region of the Venn diagram is empty.

a. If an item has Property B, then it has Property A.

b. If an item has Property A, then it has Property B.

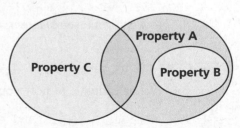

9.2   **Inductive and Deductive Reasoning** (continued)

2 **EXPLORATION:** Using a Venn Diagram (continued)

c. If an item has Property A, then it has Property C.

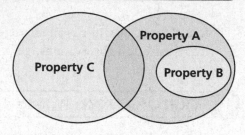

d. Some items that have Property A do not have
   Property B.

e. If an item has Property C, then it does not have Property B.

f. Some items have both Properties A and C.

g. Some items have both Properties B and C.

3 **EXPLORATION:** Reasoning and Venn Diagrams

Work with a partner. Draw a Venn diagram that shows the relationship between
different types of quadrilaterals: squares, rectangles, parallelograms, trapezoids,
rhombuses, and kites. Then write several conditional statements that are shown in your
diagram, such as "If a quadrilateral is a square, then it is a rectangle."

Communicate Your Answer

4. How can you use reasoning to solve problems?

5. Give an example of how you used reasoning to solve a real-life problem.

9.2 Notetaking with Vocabulary
For use after Lesson 9.2

In your own words, write the meaning of each vocabulary term.

conjecture

inductive reasoning

counterexample

deductive reasoning

Core Concepts

Inductive Reasoning

Recall that conjecture is an unproven statement about a general mathematical concept that is based on observations. You use **inductive reasoning** when you find a pattern in specific cases and then write a conjecture for the general case.

Notes:

Counterexample

To show that a conjecture is true, you must show that it is true for all cases. You can show that a conjecture is false, however, by finding just one *counterexample*. A **counterexample** is a specific case for which the conjecture is false.

Notes:

9.2 Notetaking with Vocabulary (continued)

Deductive Reasoning

Deductive reasoning uses facts, definitions, accepted properties, and the laws of logic to form a logical argument. This is different from *inductive reasoning*, which uses specific examples and patterns to form a conjecture.

Laws of Logic

Law of Detachment

If the hypothesis of a true conditional statement is true, then the conclusion is also true.

Law of Syllogism

If hypothesis p, then conclusion q.

If hypothesis q, then conclusion r.   If these statements are true,

If hypothesis p, then conclusion r.   then this statement is true.

Notes:

Extra Practice

In Exercises 1–4, describe the pattern. Then write or draw the next two numbers, letters, or figures.

1. 20, 19, 17, 14, 10, …

2. 2, −3, 5, −7, 11, …

3. C, E, G, I, K, …

4.

9.2 **Notetaking with Vocabulary** (continued)

In Exercises 5 and 6, make and test a conjecture about the given quantity.

5. the sum of two negative integers

6. the product of three consecutive nonzero integers

In Exercises 7 and 8, find a counterexample to show that the conjecture is false.

7. If n is a rational number, then n^2 is always less than n.

8. Line k intersects plane P at point Q on the plane. Plane P is perpendicular to line k.

In Exercises 9 and 10, use the Law of Detachment to determine what you can conclude from the given information, if possible.

9. If a triangle has equal side lengths, then each interior angle measure is $60°$. $\triangle ABC$ has equal side lengths.

10. If a quadrilateral is a rhombus, then it has two pairs of opposite sides that are parallel. Quadrilateral $PQRS$ has two pairs of opposite sides that are parallel.

In Exercises 11 and 12, use the Law of Syllogism to write a new conditional statement that follows from the pair of true statements, if possible.

11. If it does not rain, then I will walk to school.
    If I walk to school, then I will wear my walking shoes.

12. If $x > 1$, then $3x > 3$.
    If $3x > 3$, then $(3x)^2 > 9$.

9.3 Postulates and Diagrams
For use with Exploration 9.3

Essential Question In a diagram, what can be assumed and what needs to be labeled?

1 EXPLORATION: Looking at a Diagram

Work with a partner. On a piece of paper, draw two perpendicular lines. Label them $\overleftrightarrow{AB}$ and $\overleftrightarrow{CD}$. Look at the diagram from different angles. Do the lines appear perpendicular regardless of the angle at which you look at them? Describe *all* the angles at which you can look at the lines and have them appear perpendicular.

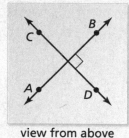

view from above

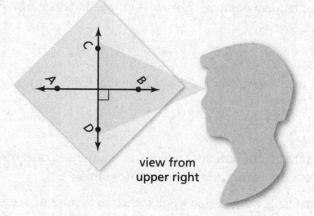

view from
upper right

2 EXPLORATION: Interpreting a Diagram

Work with a partner. When you draw a diagram, you are communicating with others. It is important that you include sufficient information in the diagram. Use the diagram to determine which of the following statements you can assume to be true. Explain your reasoning.

a. All the points shown are coplanar.

b. Points D, G, and I are collinear.

c. Points A, C, and H are collinear.

d. $\overleftrightarrow{EG}$ and $\overleftrightarrow{AH}$ are perpendicular.

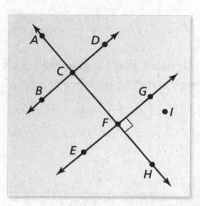

9.3 **Postulates and Diagrams** (continued)

2 **EXPLORATION: Interpreting a Diagram** (continued)

e. ∠*BCA* and ∠*ACD* are a linear pair.

f. $\overrightarrow{AF}$ and $\overrightarrow{BD}$ are perpendicular.

g. $\overrightarrow{EG}$ and $\overrightarrow{BD}$ are parallel.

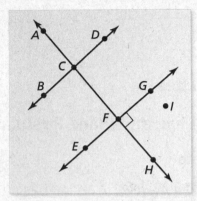

h. $\overrightarrow{AF}$ and $\overrightarrow{BD}$ are coplanar.

i. $\overrightarrow{EG}$ and $\overrightarrow{BD}$ do not intersect.

j. $\overrightarrow{AF}$ and $\overrightarrow{BD}$ intersect.

k. $\overrightarrow{EG}$ and $\overrightarrow{BD}$ are perpendicular.

l. ∠*ACD* and ∠*BCF* are vertical angles.

m. $\overrightarrow{AC}$ and $\overrightarrow{FH}$ are the same line.

Communicate Your Answer

3. In a diagram, what can be assumed and what needs to be labeled?

4. Use the diagram in Exploration 2 to write two statements you can assume to be true and two statements you cannot assume to be true. Your statements should be different from those given in Exploration 2. Explain your reasoning.

9.3 Notetaking with Vocabulary
For use after Lesson 9.3

In your own words, write the meaning of each vocabulary term.

line perpendicular to a plane

Postulates

Point, Line, and Plane Postulates

Postulate	Example	
Two Point Postulate Through any two points, there exists exactly one line.		Through points A and B, there is exactly one line ℓ. Line ℓ contains at least two points.
Line-Point Postulate A line contains at least two points.		
Line Intersection Postulate If two lines intersect, then their intersection is exactly one point.		The intersection of line m and line n is point C.
Three Point Postulate Through any three noncollinear points, there exists exactly one plane.		Through points D, E, and F, there is exactly one plane, plane R. Plane R contains at least three noncollinear points.
Plane-Point Postulate A plane contains at least three noncollinear points		

Notes:

9.3 **Notetaking with Vocabulary** (continued)

Point, Line, and Plane Postulates (continued)

Postulate	Example	
Plane-Line Postulate If two points lie in a plane, then the line containing them lies in the plane.	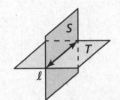	Points D and E lie in plane R, so $\overleftrightarrow{DE}$ lies in plane R.
Plane Intersection Postulate If two planes intersect, then their intersection is a line.		The intersection of plane S and plane T is line ℓ.

Notes:

Extra Practice

In Exercises 1 and 2, state the postulate illustrated by the diagram.

1.

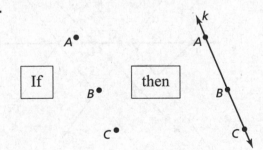

2.

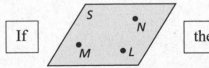 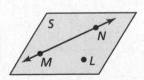

9.3 **Notetaking with Vocabulary** (continued)

In Exercises 3–6, use the diagram to write an example of the postulate.

3. Two Point Postulate

4. Line-Point Postulate

5. Plane-Point Postulate

6. Plane Intersection Postulate

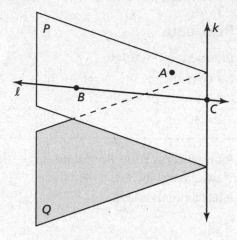

In Exercises 7 and 8, sketch a diagram of the description.

7. $\overrightarrow{RS}$ bisecting $\overline{KL}$ at point R

8. $\overleftrightarrow{AB}$ in plane U intersecting $\overleftrightarrow{CD}$ at point E, and point C not on plane U

In Exercises 9–14, use the diagram to determine whether you can assume the statement.

9. Planes A and B intersect at $\overleftrightarrow{EF}$.

10. Points C and D are collinear.

11. $\overleftrightarrow{HJ}$ and $\overrightarrow{ID}$ are perpendicular.

12. $\overleftrightarrow{GD}$ is a bisector of $\overleftrightarrow{EF}$ at point D.

13. $\overline{IH} \cong \overline{HG}$

14. $\angle HJD$ and $\angle HDJ$ are complementary angles.

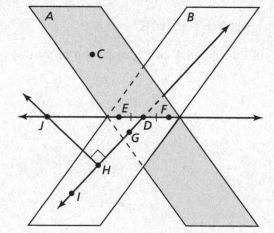

9.4 Proving Statements about Segments and Angles
For use with Exploration 9.4

Essential Question How can you prove a mathematical statement?

A **proof** is a logical argument that uses deductive reasoning to show that a statement is true.

1 EXPLORATION: Writing Reasons in a Proof

Work with a partner. Four steps of a proof are shown. Write the reasons for each statement.

Given $AC = AB + AB$

Prove $AB = BC$

STATEMENTS	REASONS
1. $AC = AB + AB$	1. Given
2. $AB + BC = AC$	2. _____
3. $AB + AB = AB + BC$	3. _____
4. $AB = BC$	4. _____

2 EXPLORATION: Writing Steps in a Proof

Work with a partner. Six steps of a proof are shown. Complete the statements that correspond to each reason.

Given $m\angle 1 = m\angle 3$

Prove $m\angle EBA = m\angle CBD$

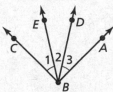

9.4 **Proving Statements about Segments and Angles** (continued)

---

2 **EXPLORATION: Writing Steps in a Proof** (continued)

STATEMENTS	REASONS
1. _____	1. Given
2. $m\angle EBA = m\angle 2 + m\angle 3$	2. Angle Addition Postulate
3. $m\angle EBA = m\angle 2 + m\angle 1$	3. Substitution Property of Equality
4. $m\angle EBA =$ _____	4. Commutative Property of Addition
5. $m\angle 1 + m\angle 2 =$ _____	5. Angle Addition Postulate
6. _____	6. Transitive Property of Equality

Communicate Your Answer

3. How can you prove a mathematical statement?

4. Use the given information and the figure to write a proof for the statement.

Given B is the midpoint of $\overline{AC}$.

C is the midpoint of $\overline{BD}$.

Prove $AB = CD$

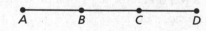

9.4 Notetaking with Vocabulary
For use after Lesson 9.4

In your own words, write the meaning of each vocabulary term.

proof

two-column proof

Core Concepts

Reflexive, Symmetric, and Transitive Properties of Equality

	Real Numbers	**Segment Lengths**	**Angle Measures**
Reflexive Property	$a = a$	$AB = AB$	$m\angle A = m\angle A$
Symmetric Property	If $a = b$, then $b = a$.	If $AB = CD$, then $CD = AB$.	If $m\angle A = m\angle B$, then $m\angle B = m\angle A$.
Transitive Property	If $a = b$ and $b = c$, then $a = c$.	If $AB = CD$ and $CD = EF$, then $AB = EF$.	If $m\angle A = m\angle B$ and $m\angle B = m\angle C$, then $m\angle A = m\angle C$.

Notes:

Theorems

Properties of Segment Congruence

Segment congruence is reflexive, symmetric, and transitive.

Reflexive   For any segment AB, $\overline{AB} \cong \overline{AB}$.

Symmetric   If $\overline{AB} \cong \overline{CD}$, then $\overline{CD} \cong \overline{AB}$.

Transitive   If $\overline{AB} \cong \overline{CD}$ and $\overline{CD} \cong \overline{EF}$, then $\overline{AB} \cong \overline{EF}$.

9.4 Notetaking with Vocabulary (continued)

Properties of Angle Congruence

Angle congruence is reflexive, symmetric, and transitive.

Reflexive   For any angle A, $\angle A \cong \angle A$.

Symmetric   If $\angle A \cong \angle B$, then $\angle B \cong \angle A$.

Transitive   If $\angle A \cong \angle B$ and $\angle B \cong \angle C$, then $\angle A \cong \angle C$.

Notes:

Writing a Two-Column Proof

In a proof, you make one statement at a time until you reach the conclusion. Because you make statements based on facts, you are using deductive reasoning. Usually the first statement-and-reason pair you write is given information.

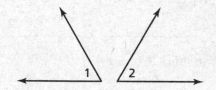

Proof of the Symmetric Property of Angle Congruence

Given $\angle 1 \cong \angle 2$ **Prove** $\angle 2 \cong \angle 1$

Copy or draw diagrams and label given information to help develop proofs. Do not mark or label the information in the Prove statement on the diagram.

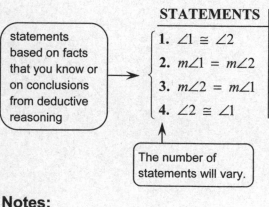

STATEMENTS	REASONS
1. $\angle 1 \cong \angle 2$	1. Given
2. $m\angle 1 = m\angle 2$	2. Definition of congruent angles
3. $m\angle 2 = m\angle 1$	3. Symmetric Property of Equality
4. $\angle 2 \cong \angle 1$	4. Definition of congruent angles

statements based on facts that you know or on conclusions from deductive reasoning

definitions, postulates, or proven theorems that allow you to state the corresponding statement

The number of statements will vary.

Remember to give a reason for the last statement.

Notes:

Name_____ Date_____

Extra Practice

In Exercises 1 and 2, complete the proof.

1. **Given** $\overline{AB}$ and $\overline{CD}$ bisect each other at point M and $\overline{BM} \cong \overline{CM}$.
   Prove $AB = AM + DM$

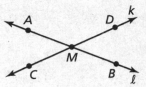

STATEMENTS	REASONS
1. $\overline{BM} \cong \overline{CM}$	1. Given
2. $\overline{CM} \cong \overline{DM}$	2. _____
3. $\overline{BM} \cong \overline{DM}$	3. _____
4. $BM = DM$	4. _____
5. _____	5. Segment Addition Postulate (Post. 1.2)
6. $AB = AM + DM$	6. _____

2. **Given** $\angle AEB$ is a complement of $\angle BEC$.
   Prove $m\angle AED = 90°$

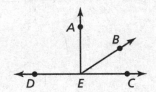

STATEMENTS	REASONS
1. $\angle AEB$ is a complement of $\angle BEC$.	1. Given
2. _____	2. Definition of complementary angles
3. $m\angle AEC = m\angle AEB + m\angle BEC$	3. _____
4. $m\angle AEC = 90°$	4. _____
5. $m\angle AED + m\angle AEC = 180°$	5. Definition of supplementary angles
6. _____	6. Substitution Property of Equality
7. $m\angle AED = 90°$	7. _____

9.4 **Notetaking with Vocabulary** (continued)

In Exercises 3 and 4, name the property that the statement illustrates.

3. If $\angle RST \cong \angle TSU$ and $\angle TSU \cong \angle VWX$, then $\angle RST \cong \angle VWX$.

4. If $\overline{GH} \cong \overline{JK}$, then $\overline{JK} \cong \overline{GH}$.

5. Write a two-column proof.

   Given M is the midpoint of $\overline{RT}$.
   Prove $MT = RS + SM$

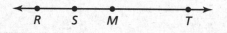

STATEMENTS	REASONS

9.5 Proving Geometric Relationships
For use with Exploration 9.5

Essential Question How can you use a flowchart to prove a mathematical statement?

1 EXPLORATION: Matching Reasons in a Flowchart Proof

Work with a partner. Match each reason with the correct step in the flowchart.

Given $AC = AB + AB$

Prove $AB = BC$

$$AC = AB + AB$$

_____

$$AB + BC = AC \longrightarrow AB + AB = AB + BC \longrightarrow AB = BC$$

_____   _____   _____

A. Segment Addition Postulate   **B.** Given

C. Transitive Property of Equality   **D.** Subtraction Property of Equality

9.5 **Proving Geometric Relationships** (continued)

---

2 **EXPLORATION:** Matching Reasons in a Flowchart Proof

Work with a partner. Match each reason with the correct step in the flowchart.

Given $m\angle 1 = m\angle 3$

Prove $m\angle EBA = m\angle CBD$

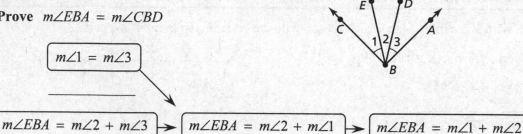

$$\boxed{m\angle 1 = m\angle 3}$$

_____

$$\boxed{m\angle EBA = m\angle 2 + m\angle 3} \rightarrow \boxed{m\angle EBA = m\angle 2 + m\angle 1} \rightarrow \boxed{m\angle EBA = m\angle 1 + m\angle 2}$$

_____   _____   _____

$$\boxed{m\angle 1 + m\angle 2 = m\angle CBD} \rightarrow \boxed{m\angle EBA = m\angle CBD}$$

_____   _____

A. Angle Addition Postulate   **B.** Transitive Property of Equality

C. Substitution Property of Equality   **D.** Angle Addition Postulate

E. Given   **F.** Commutative Property of Addition

Communicate Your Answer

3. How can you use a flowchart to prove a mathematical statement?

4. Compare the flowchart proofs above with the two-column proofs in the Section 9.4 Explorations. Explain the advantages and disadvantages of each.

9.5 Notetaking with Vocabulary
For use after Lesson 9.5

In your own words, write the meaning of each vocabulary term.

flowchart proof, or flow proof

paragraph proof

Theorems and Postulates

Right Angles Congruence Theorem

All right angles are congruent.

Notes:

Congruent Supplements Theorem

If two angles are supplementary to the same angle (or to congruent angles), then they are congruent.

If $\angle 1$ and $\angle 2$ are supplementary and $\angle 3$ and $\angle 2$ are supplementary, then $\angle 1 \cong \angle 3$.

Notes:

9.5 Notetaking with Vocabulary (continued)

Congruent Complements Theorem

If two angles are complementary to the same angle (or to congruent angles), then they are congruent.

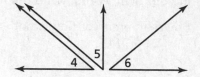

If $\angle 4$ and $\angle 5$ are complementary and $\angle 6$ and $\angle 5$ are complementary, then $\angle 4 \cong \angle 6$.

Notes:

Linear Pair Postulate

If two angles form a linear pair, then they are supplementary.

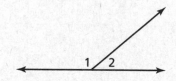

$\angle 1$ and $\angle 2$ form a linear pair, so $\angle 1$ and $\angle 2$ are supplementary and $m\angle 1 + m\angle 2 = 180°$.

Notes:

Vertical Angles Congruence Theorem

Vertical angles are congruent.

Notes:

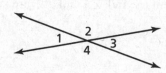

$$\angle 1 \cong \angle 3, \angle 2 \cong \angle 4$$

9.5 **Notetaking with Vocabulary** (continued)

Extra Practice

1. Complete the flowchart proof. Then write a two-column proof.

   Given $\angle ACB$ and $\angle ACD$ are supplementary.

   $\angle EGF$ and $\angle ACD$ are supplementary.

   Prove $\angle ACB \cong \angle EGF$

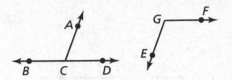

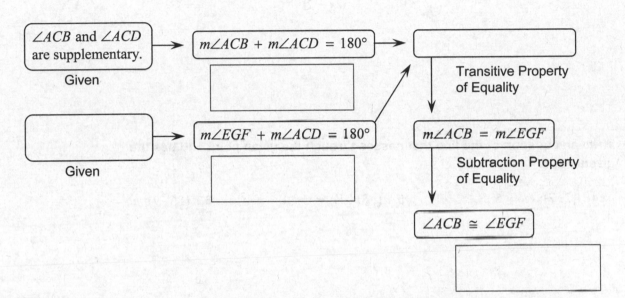

Two-Column Proof

STATEMENTS	REASONS

Name _____ Date _____

Find the measure of each angle.

1.

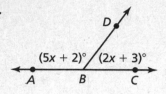

$(5x + 2)°$ $(2x + 3)°$

A   B   C

2.

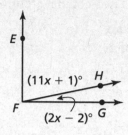

E

$(11x + 1)°$ H

F

$(2x - 2)°$ G

3.

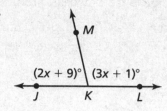

M

$(2x + 9)°$ $(3x + 1)°$

J   K   L

Write an equation of the line that passes through the given point and has the given slope.

4. $(2, 7)$; $m = 5$

5. $(-8, -1)$; $m = \dfrac{3}{4}$

6. $(5, -9)$; $m = \dfrac{1}{6}$

7. $(0, -8)$; $m = \dfrac{3}{5}$

8. $(-4, 3)$; $m = \dfrac{1}{3}$

9. $(2, -1)$; $m = 5$

10.1 Pairs of Lines and Angles
For use with Exploration 10.1

Essential Question What does it mean when two lines are parallel, intersecting, coincident, or skew?

1 EXPLORATION: Points of Intersection

Work with a partner. Write the number of points of intersection of each pair of coplanar lines.

a. parallel lines

b. intersecting lines

c. coincident lines

_____   _____   _____

2 EXPLORATION: Classifying Pairs of Lines

Work with a partner. The figure shows a *right rectangular prism*. All its angles are right angles. Classify each of the following pairs of lines as *parallel, intersecting, coincident,* or *skew*. Justify your answers. (Two lines are **skew lines** when they do not intersect and are not coplanar.)

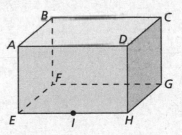

Pair of Lines	Classification	Reason
a. $\overleftrightarrow{AB}$ and $\overleftrightarrow{BC}$		
b. $\overleftrightarrow{AD}$ and $\overleftrightarrow{BC}$		
c. $\overleftrightarrow{EI}$ and $\overleftrightarrow{IH}$		
d. $\overleftrightarrow{BF}$ and $\overleftrightarrow{EH}$		
e. $\overleftrightarrow{EF}$ and $\overleftrightarrow{CG}$		
f. $\overleftrightarrow{AB}$ and $\overleftrightarrow{GH}$		

10.1 **Pairs of Lines and Angles** (continued)

---

3 **EXPLORATION: Identifying Pairs of Angles**

Work with a partner. In the figure, two parallel lines are intersected by a third line called a *transversal*.

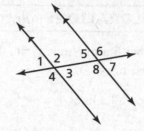

a. Identify all the pairs of vertical angles. Explain your reasoning.

b. Identify all the linear pairs of angles. Explain your reasoning.

Communicate Your Answer

4. What does it mean when two lines are parallel, intersecting, coincident, or skew?

5. In Exploration 2, find three more pairs of lines that are different from those given. Classify the pairs of lines as *parallel, intersecting, coincident,* or *skew*. Justify your answers.

Name ____ Date __________

10.1 Notetaking with Vocabulary
For use after Lesson 10.1

In your own words, write the meaning of each vocabulary term.

skew lines

parallel planes

transversal

corresponding angles

alternate interior angles

alternate exterior angles

consecutive interior angles

Notes:

10.1 Notetaking with Vocabulary (continued)

Core Concepts

Parallel Lines, Skew Lines, and Parallel Planes

Two lines that do not intersect are either *parallel lines* or *skew lines*. Recall that two lines are parallel lines when they do not intersect and are coplanar. Two lines are **skew lines** when they do not intersect and are not coplanar. Also, two planes that do not intersect are **parallel planes**.

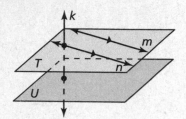

Lines m and n are parallel lines $(m \parallel n)$.

Lines m and k are skew lines.

Planes T and U are parallel planes $(T \parallel U)$.

Lines k and n are intersecting lines, and there is a plane (not shown) containing them.

Small directed arrows, as shown on lines m and n above, are used to show that lines are parallel. The symbol $\parallel$ means "is parallel to," as in $m \parallel n$.

Segments and rays are parallel when they lie in parallel lines. A line is parallel to a plane when the line is in a plane parallel to the given plane. In the diagram above, line n is parallel to plane U.

Notes:

Parallel Postulate

If there is a line and a point not on the line, then there is exactly one line through the point parallel to the given line.

There is exactly one line through P parallel to ℓ.

Notes:

10.1 **Notetaking with Vocabulary** (continued)

Perpendicular Postulate

If there is a line and a point not on the line, then there is exactly one line through the point perpendicular to the given line.

There is exactly one line through P perpendicular to ℓ.

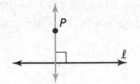

Notes:

Angles Formed by Transversals

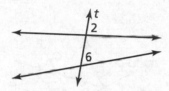

Two angles are **corresponding angles** when they have corresponding positions. For example, $\angle 2$ and $\angle 6$ are above the lines and to the right of the transversal t.

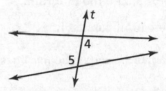

Two angles are **alternate interior angles** when they lie between the two lines and on opposite sides of the transversal t.

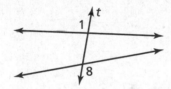

Two angles are **alternate exterior angles** when they lie outside the two lines and on opposite sides of the transversal t.

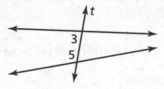

Two angles are **consecutive interior angles** when they lie between the two lines and on the same side of the transversal t.

Notes:

10.1 Notetaking with Vocabulary (continued)

Extra Practice

In Exercises 1–4, think of each segment in the diagram as part of a line.
Which line(s) or plane(s) contain point *B* and appear to fit the description?

1. line(s) skew to $\overleftrightarrow{FG}$.

2. line(s) perpendicular to $\overleftrightarrow{FG}$.

3. line(s) parallel to $\overleftrightarrow{FG}$.

4. plane(s) parallel to plane *FGH*.

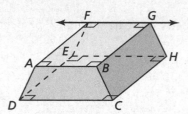

In Exercises 5–8, use the diagram.

5. Name a pair of parallel lines.

6. Name a pair of perpendicular lines.

7. Is $\overleftrightarrow{WX} \parallel \overleftrightarrow{QR}$? Explain.

8. Is $\overleftrightarrow{ST} \perp \overleftrightarrow{NV}$? Explain.

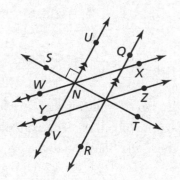

In Exercises 9–12, identify all pairs of angles of the given type.

9. corresponding

10. alternate interior

11. alternate exterior

12. consecutive interior

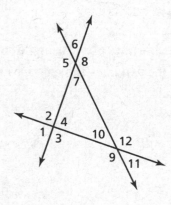

10.2 Parallel Lines and Transversals
For use with Exploration 10.2

Essential Question When two parallel lines are cut by a transversal, which of the resulting pairs of angles are congruent?

---

1 **EXPLORATION:** Exploring Parallel Lines

Go to *BigIdeasMath.com* for an interactive tool to investigate this exploration.

Work with a partner.
Use dynamic geometry software to draw two parallel lines. Draw a third line that intersects both parallel lines. Find the measures of the eight angles that are formed. What can you conclude?

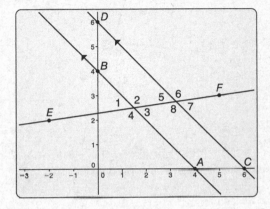

---

2 **EXPLORATION:** Writing Conjectures

Work with a partner. Use the results of Exploration 1 to write conjectures about the following pairs of angles formed by two parallel lines and a transversal.

a. corresponding angles

b. alternate interior angles

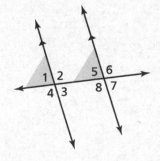

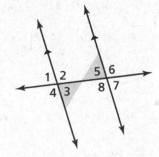

10.2 **Parallel Lines and Transversals** (continued)

---

2 **EXPLORATION: Writing Conjectures** (continued)

c. alternate exterior angles

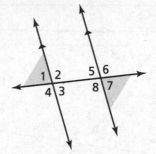

d. consecutive interior angles

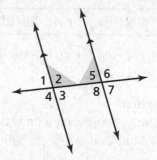

Communicate Your Answer

3. When two parallel lines are cut by a transversal, which of the resulting pairs of angles are congruent?

4. In Exploration 2, $m\angle 1 = 80°$. Find the other angle measures.

10.2 Notetaking with Vocabulary
For use after Lesson 10.2

In your own words, write the meaning of each vocabulary term.

corresponding angles

parallel lines

supplementary angles

vertical angles

Theorems

Corresponding Angles Theorem

If two parallel lines are cut by a transversal, then the pairs of corresponding angles are congruent.

Examples   In the diagram, $\angle 2 \cong \angle 6$ and $\angle 3 \cong \angle 7$.

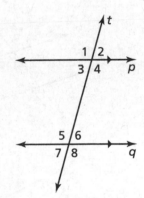

Alternate Interior Angles Theorem

If two parallel lines are cut by a transversal, then the pairs of alternate interior angles are congruent.

Examples   In the diagram, $\angle 3 \cong \angle 6$ and $\angle 4 \cong \angle 5$.

Alternate Exterior Angles Theorem

If two parallel lines are cut by a transversal, then the pairs of alternate exterior angles are congruent.

Examples   In the diagram, $\angle 1 \cong \angle 8$ and $\angle 2 \cong \angle 7$.

10.2 Notetaking with Vocabulary (continued)

Consecutive Interior Angles Theorem

If two parallel lines are cut by a transversal, then the pairs of consecutive interior angles are supplementary.

Examples In the diagram, $\angle 3$ and $\angle 5$ are supplementary, and $\angle 4$ and $\angle 6$ are supplementary.

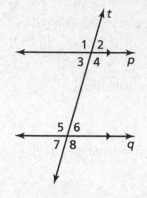

Notes:

Extra Practice

In Exercises 1–4, find $m\angle 1$ and $m\angle 2$. Tell which theorem you use in each case.

1.

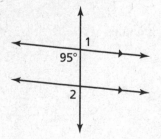

2.

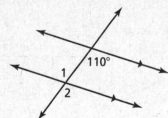

3.

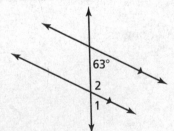

10.2 **Notetaking with Vocabulary** (continued)

4.

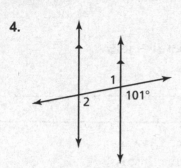

In Exercises 5–8, find the value of *x*. Show your steps.

5.

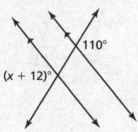

6.

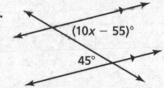

7.

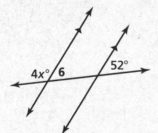

8.

10.3 Proofs with Parallel Lines
For use with Exploration 10.3

Essential Question For which of the theorems involving parallel lines and transversals is the converse true?

---

1 EXPLORATION: Exploring Converses

Work with a partner. Write the converse of each conditional statement. Draw a diagram to represent the converse. Determine whether the converse is true. Justify your conclusion.

a. Corresponding Angles Theorem

If two parallel lines are cut by a transversal, then the pairs of corresponding angles are congruent.

Converse

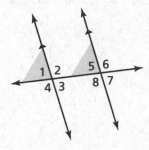

b. Alternate Interior Angles Theorem

If two parallel lines are cut by a transversal, then the pairs of alternate interior angles are congruent.

Converse

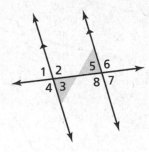

c. Alternate Exterior Angles Theorem

If two parallel lines are cut by a transversal, then the pairs of alternate exterior angles are congruent.

Converse

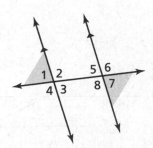

10.3 **Proofs with Parallel Lines** (continued)

---

1 **EXPLORATION: Exploring Converses** (continued)

d. **Consecutive Interior Angles Theorem**

If two parallel lines are cut by a transversal, then the pairs of consecutive interior angles are supplementary.

Converse

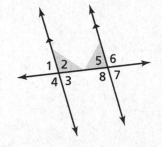

Communicate Your Answer

2. For which of the theorems involving parallel lines and transversals is the converse true?

3. In Exploration 1, explain how you would prove any of the theorems that you found to be true.

10.3 Notetaking with Vocabulary
For use after Lesson 10.3

In your own words, write the meaning of each vocabulary term.

converse

parallel lines

transversal

corresponding angles

congruent

alternate interior angles

alternate exterior angles

consecutive interior angles

Theorems

Corresponding Angles Converse

If two lines are cut by a transversal so the corresponding angles
are congruent, then the lines are parallel.

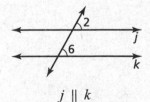

$j \parallel k$

Notes:

10.3 Notetaking with Vocabulary (continued)

Alternate Interior Angles Converse

If two lines are cut by a transversal so the alternate interior angles
are congruent, then the lines are parallel.

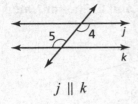

$j \parallel k$

Notes:

Alternate Exterior Angles Converse

If two lines are cut by a transversal so the alternate exterior angles are
congruent, then the lines are parallel.

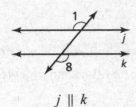

$j \parallel k$

Notes:

Consecutive Interior Angles Converse

If two lines are cut by a transversal so the consecutive interior angles are
supplementary, then the lines are parallel.

Notes:

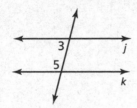

If $\angle 3$ and $\angle 5$ are
supplementary, then $j \parallel k$.

Transitive Property of Parallel Lines

If two lines are parallel to the same line, then they are parallel to each other.

Notes:

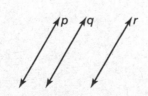

If $p \parallel q$ and $q \parallel r$, then
$p \parallel r$.

10.3 Notetaking with Vocabulary (continued)

Extra Practice

In Exercises 1 and 2, find the value of *x* that makes *m* ∥ *n*. Explain your reasoning.

1.

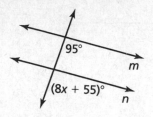

2.

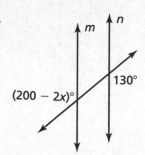

In Exercises 3–6, decide whether there is enough information to prove that *m* ∥ *n*.
If so, state the theorem you would use.

3.

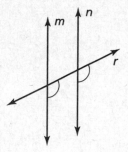

4.

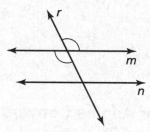

5.

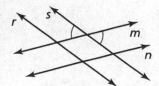

6.

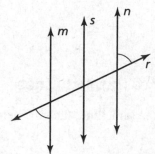

10.4 **Proofs with Perpendicular Lines**
For use with Exploration 10.4

Essential Question What conjectures can you make about perpendicular lines?

---

1 EXPLORATION: Writing Conjectures

Work with a partner. Fold a piece of paper in half twice. Label points on the two creases, as shown.

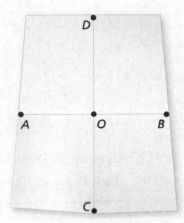

a. Write a conjecture about $\overline{AB}$ and $\overline{CD}$. Justify your conjecture.

b. Write a conjecture about $\overline{AO}$ and $\overline{OB}$. Justify your conjecture.

---

2 EXPLORATION: Exploring a Segment Bisector

Work with a partner. Fold and crease a piece of paper, as shown. Label the ends of the crease as A and B.

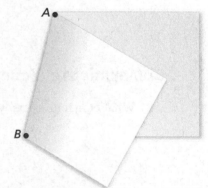

a. Fold the paper again so that point A coincides with point B. Crease the paper on that fold.

b. Unfold the paper and examine the four angles formed by the two creases. What can you conclude about the four angles?

10.4 **Proofs with Perpendicular Lines** (continued)

3 EXPLORATION: Writing a Conjecture

Go to *BigIdeasMath.com* for an interactive tool to investigate this exploration.

Work with a partner.

a. Draw $\overline{AB}$, as shown.

b. Draw an arc with center A on each side of $\overline{AB}$. Using the same compass setting, draw an arc with center B on each side of $\overline{AB}$. Label the intersections of the arcs C and D.

c. Draw $\overline{CD}$. Label its intersection with $\overline{AB}$ as O. Write a conjecture about the resulting diagram. Justify your conjecture.

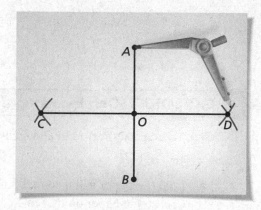

Communicate Your Answer

4. What conjectures can you make about perpendicular lines?

5. In Exploration 3, find AO and OB when $AB = 4$ units.

10.4 Notetaking with Vocabulary
For use after Lesson 10.4

In your own words, write the meaning of each vocabulary term.

distance from a point to a line

perpendicular bisector

Theorems

Linear Pair Perpendicular Theorem

If two lines intersect to form a linear pair of congruent angles, then the lines are perpendicular.

If $\angle 1 \cong \angle 2$, then $g \perp h$.

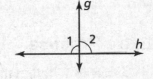

Notes:

Perpendicular Transversal Theorem

In a plane, if a transversal is perpendicular to one of two parallel lines, then it is perpendicular to the other line.

If $h \parallel k$ and $j \perp h$, then $j \perp k$.

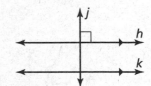

Notes:

10.4 Notetaking with Vocabulary (continued)

Lines Perpendicular to a Transversal Theorem

In a plane, if two lines are perpendicular to the same line, then they are parallel to each other.

If $m \perp p$ and $n \perp p$, then $m \parallel n$.

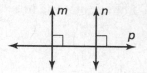

Notes:

Extra Practice

In Exercises 1–4, find the distance from point A to $\overleftrightarrow{BC}$.

1.

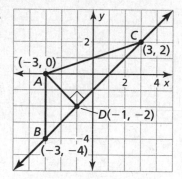

2.

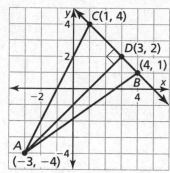

3.

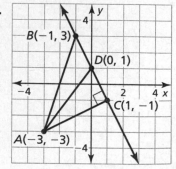

4.

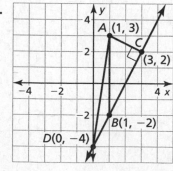

10.4 **Notetaking with Vocabulary** (continued)

In Exercises 5–8, determine which lines, if any, must be parallel. Explain your reasoning.

5.

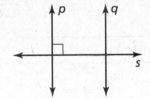

6.

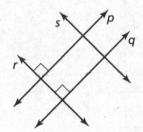

7.

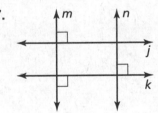

8.

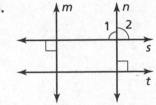

10.5 Using Parallel and Perpendicular Lines
For use with Exploration 10.5

Essential Question How can you find the distance between two parallel lines?

1 EXPLORATION: Finding the Distance Between Two Parallel Lines

Work with a partner.

a. Draw a line and label it ℓ. Draw a point not on line ℓ and label it P.

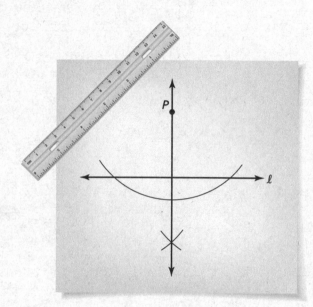

b. Construct a line through point P perpendicular to line ℓ.

c. Use a centimeter ruler to measure the distance from point P to line ℓ.

10.5 Using Parallel and Perpendicular Lines (continued)

d. Construct a line through point P parallel to line ℓ and label it m.

e. Choose any point except point P on either line and label it Q. Describe how to find the distance from point Q to the other line.

f. Find the distance from point Q to the other line. Compare this distance to the distance from point P to line ℓ.

g. Is the distance from any point on line ℓ to line m constant? Explain your reasoning.

Communicate Your Answer

2. How can you find the distance between two parallel lines?

3. Use centimeter graph paper and a centimeter ruler to find the distance between the two parallel lines.

a. $y = 2x + 2$
$y = 2x - 7$

b. $y = -x + 4$
$y = -x - 5$

10.5 Notetaking with Vocabulary
For use after Lesson 10.5

Theorems

Slopes of Parallel Lines

In a coordinate plane, two distinct nonvertical lines are parallel if and only if they have the same slope.

Any two vertical lines are parallel.

Notes:

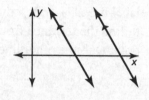

$$m_1 = m_2$$

Slopes of Perpendicular Lines

In a coordinate plane, two nonvertical lines are perpendicular if and only if the product of their slopes is -1.

Horizontal lines are perpendicular to vertical lines.

Notes:

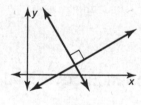

$$m_1 \bullet m_2 = -1$$

10.5 Notetaking with Vocabulary (continued)

Extra Practice

In Exercises 1–5, find the distance from point A to the given line.

1.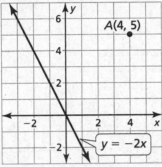

2.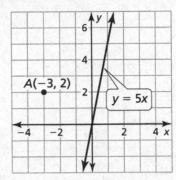

3. $A(0, 5), y = -3x - 5$

4. $A(9, 12), y = x - 3$

5. $A(7, -3)$, line with slope of 4 that passes through $(-2, -5)$

10.5   **Notetaking with Vocabulary** (continued)

In Exercises 6–10, find the distance between the parallel lines.

6.

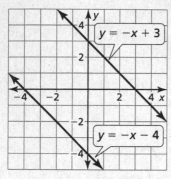

$y = -x + 3$

$y = -x - 4$

7.

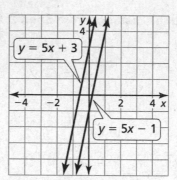

$y = 5x + 3$

$y = 5x - 1$

8. $y = 4x - 6, y = 4x - 10$

9. $y = -7x + 3, y = -7x - 9$

10. $y = \dfrac{3}{4}x - 3,$ parallel line that passes through $(-2, 5)$

Chapter 11 **Maintaining Mathematical Proficiency**

Tell whether the shaded figure is a translation, reflection, or rotation of the nonshaded figure.

1.

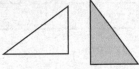

2.

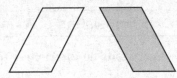

3.

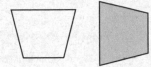

4.

Find the perimeter and area of the polygon with the given vertices.

5. $A(-4, 5), B(2, 5), C(2, -1), D(-4, -1)$

6. $E(0, 3), F(-3, 7), G(0, 7)$

11.1 Translations

For use with Exploration 11.1

Essential Question   How can you translate a figure in a coordinate plane?

---

1   EXPLORATION: Translating a Triangle in a Coordinate Plane

Go to *BigIdeasMath.com* for an interactive tool to investigate this exploration.

Work with a partner.

  a. Use dynamic geometry software to draw any triangle and label it $\triangle ABC$.

  b. Copy the triangle and *translate* (or slide) it to form a new figure, called an *image*, $\triangle A'B'C'$. (read as "triangle A prime, B prime, C prime").

  c. What is the relationship between the coordinates of the vertices of $\triangle ABC$ and those of $\triangle A'B'C'$?

  d. What do you observe about the side lengths and angle measures of the two triangles?

Sample

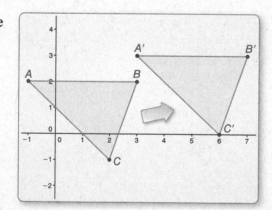

---

2   EXPLORATION: Translating a Triangle in a Coordinate Plane

Go to *BigIdeasMath.com* for an interactive tool to investigate this exploration.

Work with a partner.

  a. The point (x, y) is translated a units horizontally and b units vertically. Write a rule to determine the coordinates of the image of (x, y).

$$(x, y) \rightarrow (\underline{\hspace{1cm}}, \underline{\hspace{1cm}})$$

11.1 **Translations** (continued)

b. Use the rule you wrote in part (a) to translate △ABC
4 units left and 3 units down. What are the coordinates
of the vertices of the image, △A′B′C′?

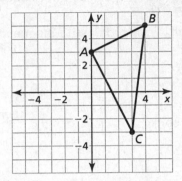

c. Draw △A′B′C′. Are its side lengths the same as those of
△ABC? Justify your answer.

3 **EXPLORATION:** Comparing Angles of Translations

Work with a partner.

a. In Exploration 2, is △ABC a right triangle? Justify your answer.

b. In Exploration 2, is △A′B′C′ a right triangle? Justify your answer.

c. Do you think translations always preserve angle measures? Explain your
reasoning.

Communicate Your Answer

4. How can you translate a figure in a coordinate plane?

5. In Exploration 2, translate △A′B′C′ 3 units right and 4 units up. What are the
coordinates of the vertices of the image, △A″B″C″? How are these coordinates
related to the coordinates of the vertices of the original triangle, △ABC?

Name ______________________ Date __________

11.1 Notetaking with Vocabulary

For use after Lesson 11.1

In your own words, write the meaning of each vocabulary term.

vector

initial point

terminal point

horizontal component

vertical component

component form

transformation

image

preimage

translation

rigid motion

composition of transformations

11.1 Notetaking with Vocabulary (continued)

Core Concepts

Vectors

The diagram shows a vector. The **initial point**, or starting point, of the vector is P, and the **terminal point**, or ending point, is Q. The vector is named $\overrightarrow{PQ}$, which is read as "vector PQ." The **horizontal component** of $\overrightarrow{PQ}$ is 5, and the **vertical component** is 3. The **component form** of a vector combines the horizontal and vertical components. So, the component form of $\overrightarrow{PQ}$ is $\langle 5, 3 \rangle$.

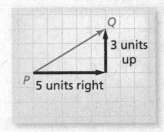

Notes:

Translations

A **translation** moves every point of a figure the same distance in the same direction. More specifically, a translation *maps*, or moves, the points P and Q of a plane figure along a vector $\langle a, b \rangle$ to the points P' and Q', so that one of the following statements is true.

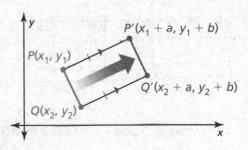

- $PP' = QQ'$ and $\overline{PP'} \parallel \overline{QQ'}$, or

- $PP' = QQ'$ and $\overline{PP'}$ and $\overline{QQ'}$ are collinear.

Notes:

Extra Practice

In Exercises 1–3, name the vector and write its component form.

1.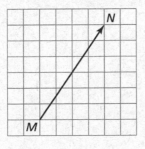

2.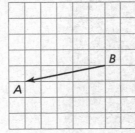

3.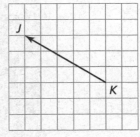

11.1 **Notetaking with Vocabulary** (continued)

In Exercises 4–7, the vertices of △*ABC* are *A*(1, 2), *B*(5, 1), *C*(5, 4).
Translate △*ABC* using the given vector. Graph △*ABC* and its image.

4. $\langle -4, 0 \rangle$

5. $\langle -2, -4 \rangle$

6. $\langle 0, -5 \rangle$

7. $\langle 1, -3 \rangle$

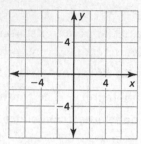

In Exercises 8 and 9, write a rule for the translation of quadrilateral *PQRS* to
quadrilateral *P′Q′R′S′*.

8.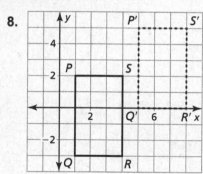

9.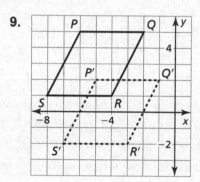

In Exercises 10 and 11, use the translation.

$(x, y) \rightarrow (x + 6, y - 3)$

10. What is the image of $J(4, 5)$?

11. What is the image of $R'(0, -5)$?

12. In a video game, you move a spaceship 1 unit left and 4 units up. Then, you move
the spaceship 2 units left. Rewrite the composition as a single transformation.

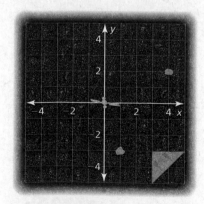

11.2 Reflections
For use with Exploration 11.2

Essential Question How can you reflect a figure in a coordinate plane?

1 **EXPLORATION: Reflecting a Triangle Using a Reflective Device**

Work with a partner. Use a straightedge to draw any triangle on paper. Label it $\triangle ABC$.

a. Use the straightedge to draw a line that does not pass through the triangle. Label it m.

b. Place a reflective device on line m.

c. Use the reflective device to plot the images of the vertices of $\triangle ABC$. Label the images of vertices A, B, and C as A', B', and C', respectively.

d. Use a straightedge to draw $\triangle A'B'C'$ by connecting the vertices.

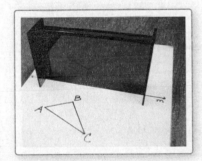

11.2 **Reflections** (continued)

2 **EXPLORATION: Reflecting a Triangle in a Coordinate Plane**

Go to *BigIdeasMath.com* for an interactive tool to investigate this exploration.

Work with a partner. Use dynamic geometry software to draw any triangle and label it $\triangle ABC$.

   a. *Reflect* $\triangle ABC$ in the *y*-axis to form $\triangle A'B'C'$.

   b. What is the relationship between the coordinates of the vertices of $\triangle ABC$ and those of $\triangle A'B'C'$?

   c. What do you observe about the side lengths and angle measures of the two triangles?

   d. *Reflect* $\triangle ABC$ in the *x*-axis to form $\triangle A'B'C'$. Then repeat parts (b) and (c).

Communicate Your Answer

   3. How can you reflect a figure in a coordinate plane?

Name_____ Date_____

In your own words, write the meaning of each vocabulary term.

reflection

line of reflection

glide reflection

line symmetry

line of symmetry

Core Concepts

Reflections

A **reflection** is a transformation that uses a line like a mirror to reflect a figure. The mirror line is called the **line of reflection**.

A reflection in a line m maps every point P in the plane to a point P', so that for each point on of the following properties is true.

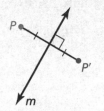

point P not on m point P on m

- If P is not m, then m is the perpendicular bisector of $\overline{PP'}$, or

- If P is on m, then $P = P'$.

Notes:

11.2 Notetaking with Vocabulary (continued)

Core Concepts

Coordinate Rules for Reflections

- If (a, b) is reflected in the x-axis, then its image is the point $(a, -b)$.

- If (a, b) is reflected in the y-axis, then its image is the point $(-a, b)$.

- If (a, b) is reflected in the line $y = x$, then its image is the point (b, a).

- If (a, b) is reflected in the line $y = -x$, then its image is the point $(-b, -a)$.

Notes:

Reflection Postulate

A reflection is a rigid motion.

Extra Practice

In Exercises 1–4, graph △ABC and its image after a reflection in the given line.

1. $A(-1, 5)$, $B(-4, 4)$, $C(-3, 1)$; y-axis

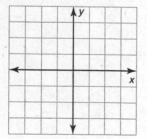

2. $A(0, 2)$, $B(4, 5)$, $C(5, 2)$; x-axis

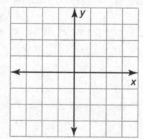

3. $A(2, -1)$, $B(-4, -2)$, $C(-1, -3)$; $y = 1$

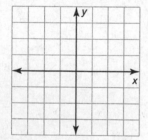

4. $A(-2, 3)$, $B(-2, -2)$, $C(0, -2)$; $x = -3$

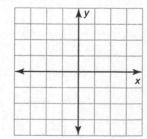

11.2 **Notetaking with Vocabulary** (continued)

In Exercises 5 and 6, graph the polygon's image after a reflection in the given line.

5. $y = x$

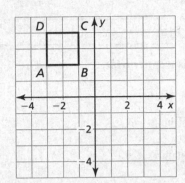

6. $y = -x$

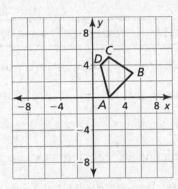

In Exercises 7 and 8, graph $\triangle JKL$ **with vertices** $J(3, 1)$, $K(4, 2)$, **and** $L(1, 3)$ **and its image after the glide reflection.**

7. **Translation:** $(x, y) \rightarrow (x - 6, y - 1)$

   Reflection: in the line $y = -x$

8. **Translation:** $(x, y) \rightarrow (x, y - 4)$

   Reflection: in the line $x = 1$

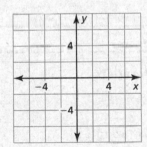

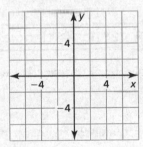

In Exercises 9–12, identify the line symmetry (if any) of the word.

9. MOON   10. WOW   11. KID   12. DOCK

13. You are placing a power strip along wall w that connects to two computers. Where should you place the power strip to minimize the length of the connecting cables?

Computer A

Computer B

w

11.3 Rotations
For use with Exploration 11.3

Essential Question How can you rotate a figure in a coordinate plane?

---

1 **EXPLORATION: Rotating a Triangle in a Coordinate Plane**

Go to BigIdeasMath.com for an interactive tool to investigate this exploration.

Work with a partner.

    a. Use dynamic geometry software to draw any triangle and label it $\triangle ABC$.

    b. *Rotate* the triangle 90° counterclockwise about the origin to form $\triangle A'B'C'$.

    c. What is the relationship between the coordinates of the vertices of $\triangle ABC$ and those of $\triangle A'B'C'$?

    d. What do you observe about the side lengths and angle measures of the two triangles?

---

2 **EXPLORATION: Rotating a Triangle in a Coordinate Plane**

Go to BigIdeasMath.com for an interactive tool to investigate this exploration.

Work with a partner.

    a. The point (x, y) is rotated 90° counterclockwise about the origin. Write a rule to determine the coordinates of the image of (x, y).

    b. Use the rule you wrote in part (a) to rotate $\triangle ABC$ 90° counterclockwise about the origin. What are the coordinates of the vertices of the image, $\triangle A'B'C'$?

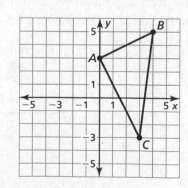

    c. Draw $\triangle A'B'C'$. Are its side lengths the same as those of $\triangle ABC$? Justify your answer.

11.3   **Rotations (continued)**

---

3   **EXPLORATION:** Rotating a Triangle in a Coordinate Plane

Work with a partner.

a. The point (x, y) is rotated 180° counterclockwise about the origin. Write a rule to determine the coordinates of the image of (x, y). Explain how you found the rule.

b. Use the rule you wrote in part (a) to rotate $\triangle ABC$ (from Exploration 2) 180° counterclockwise about the origin. What are the coordinates of the vertices of the image, $\triangle A'B'C'$?

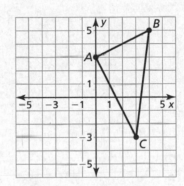

Communicate Your Answer

4. How can you rotate a figure in a coordinate plane?

5. In Exploration 3, rotate $\triangle A'B'C'$ 180° counterclockwise about the origin. What are the coordinates of the vertices of the image, $\triangle A''B''C''$? How are these coordinates related to the coordinates of the vertices of the original triangle, $\triangle ABC$?

11.3 Notetaking with Vocabulary
For use after Lesson 11.3

In your own words, write the meaning of each vocabulary term.

rotation

center of rotation

angle of rotation

rotational symmetry

center of symmetry

Core Concepts

Rotations

A **rotation** is a transformation in which a figure is turned about a fixed point called the **center of rotation**. Rays drawn from the center of rotation to a point and its image form the **angle of rotation**.

A rotation about a point P through an angle of $x°$ maps every point Q in the plane to a point Q', so that one of the following properties is true.

- If Q is not the center of rotation P, then $QP = Q'P$ and $m\angle QPQ' = x°$, or

- If Q is the center of rotation P, then $Q = Q'$.

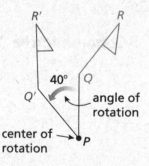

Notes:

11.3 Notetaking with Vocabulary (continued)

Coordinate Rules for Rotations about the Origin

When a point (a, b) is rotated counterclockwise about the origin, the following are true.

- For a rotation of 90°, $(a, b) \rightarrow (-b, a)$.
- For a rotation of 180°, $(a, b) \rightarrow (-a, -b)$.
- For a rotation of 270°, $(a, b) \rightarrow (b, -a)$.

Notes:

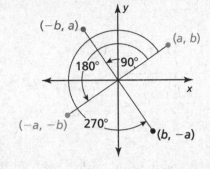

Rotation Postulate

A rotation is a rigid motion.

Extra Practice

In Exercises 1–3, graph the image of the polygon after a rotation of the given number of degrees about the origin.

1. 180°

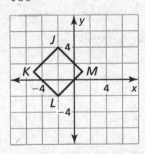

2. 90°

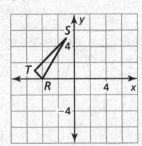

3. 270°

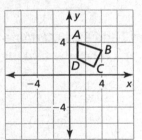

In Exercises 4–7, graph the image of $\overline{MN}$ after the composition.

4. Reflection: x-axis

Rotation: 180° about the origin

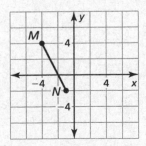

5. Rotation: 90° about the origin

Translation: $(x, y) \rightarrow (x + 2, y - 3)$

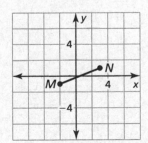

11.3 Notetaking with Vocabulary (continued)

6. **Rotation:** $270°$ about the origin

   Reflection: in the line $y = x$

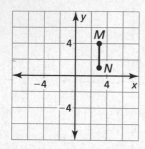

7. **Rotation:** $90°$ about the origin

   Translation: $(x, y) \rightarrow (x - 5, y)$

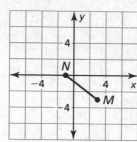

In Exercises 8 and 9, graph $\triangle JKL$ with vertices $J(2, 3)$, $K(1, -1)$, and $L(-1, 0)$ and its image after the composition.

8. **Rotation:** $180°$ about the origin

   Reflection: $x = 2$

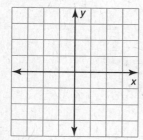

9. **Translation:** $(x, y) \rightarrow (x - 4, y - 4)$

   Rotation: $270°$ about the origin

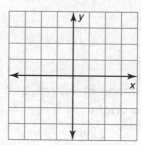

In Exercises 10 and 11, determine whether the figure has rotational symmetry. If so, describe any rotations that map the figure onto itself.

10.

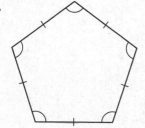

11.

11.4 Congruence and Transformations
For use with Exploration 11.4

Essential Question What conjectures can you make about a figure reflected in two lines?

1 EXPLORATION: Reflections in Parallel Lines

Go to _BigIdeasMath.com_ for an interactive tool to investigate this exploration.

Work with a partner. Use dynamic geometry software to draw any scalene triangle and label it $\triangle ABC$.

a. Draw any line $\overleftrightarrow{DE}$. Reflect $\triangle ABC$ in $\overleftrightarrow{DE}$ to form $\triangle A'B'C'$.

b. Draw a line parallel to $\overleftrightarrow{DE}$. Reflect $\triangle A'B'C'$ in the new line to form $\triangle A''B''C''$.

c. Draw the line through point A that is perpendicular to $\overleftrightarrow{DE}$. What do you notice?

d. Find the distance between points A and A''. Find the distance between the two parallel lines. What do you notice?

e. Hide $\triangle A'B'C'$. Is there a single transformation that maps $\triangle ABC$ to $\triangle A''B''C''$. Explain.

f. Make conjectures based on your answers in parts (c)–(e). Test your conjectures by changing $\triangle ABC$ and the parallel lines.

11.4 **Congruence and Transformations** (continued)

---

2 **EXPLORATION:** Reflections in Intersecting Lines

Go to *BigIdeasMath.com* for an interactive tool to investigate this exploration.

Work with a partner. Use dynamic geometry software to draw any scalene triangle and label it $\triangle ABC$.

  a. Draw any line $\overleftrightarrow{DE}$. Reflect $\triangle ABC$ in $\overleftrightarrow{DE}$ to form $\triangle A'B'C'$.

  b. Draw any line $\overleftrightarrow{DF}$ so that $\angle EDF$ is less than or equal to 90°. Reflect $\triangle A'B'C'$ in $\overleftrightarrow{DF}$ to form $\triangle A''B''C''$.

  c. Find the measure of $\angle EDF$. Rotate $\triangle ABC$ counterclockwise about point D twice using the measure of $\angle EDF$.

  d. Make a conjecture about a figure reflected in two intersecting lines. Test your conjecture by changing $\triangle ABC$ and the lines.

Communicate Your Answer

  3. What conjectures can you make about a figure reflected in two lines?

  4. Point Q is reflected in two parallel lines, $\overleftrightarrow{GH}$ and $\overleftrightarrow{JK}$, to form Q' and Q''. The distance from $\overleftrightarrow{GH}$ to $\overleftrightarrow{JK}$ is 3.2 inches. What is the distance QQ''?

11.4 Notetaking with Vocabulary
For use after Lesson 11.4

In your own words, write the meaning of each vocabulary term.

congruent figures

congruence transformation

Theorems

Reflections in Parallel Lines Theorem

If lines k and m are parallel, then a reflection in line k followed by a reflection in line m is the same as a translation.

If A'' is the image of A, then

1. $\overline{AA''}$ is perpendicular to k and m, and

2. $AA'' = 2d$, where d is the distance between k and m.

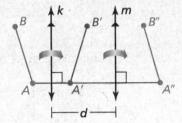

Notes:

Reflections in Intersecting Lines Theorem

If lines k and m intersect at point P, then a reflection in line k followed by a reflection in line m is the same as a rotation about point P.

The angle of rotation is $2x°$, where $x°$ is the measure of the acute or right angle formed by lines k and m.

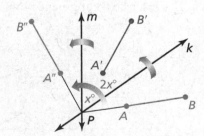

Notes:

11.4 **Notetaking with Vocabulary** (continued)

Extra Practice

1. Identify any congruent figures in the coordinate plane. Explain.

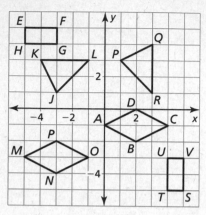

2. Describe a congruence transformation that maps △PQR to △STU.

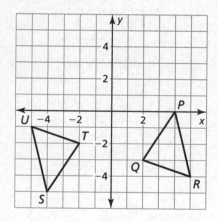

3. Describe a congruence transformation that maps polygon *ABCD* to polygon *EFGH*.

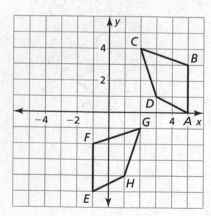

11.4 **Notetaking with Vocabulary** (continued)

In Exercises 4 and 5, determine whether the polygons with the given vertices are congruent. Use transformations to explain your reasoning.

4. $A(2, 2)$, $B(3, 1)$, $C(1, 1)$ and
   $D(2, -2)$, $E(3, -1)$, $F(1, -1)$

5. $G(3, 3)$, $H(2, 1)$, $I(6, 2)$, $J(6, 3)$ and
   $K(2, -1)$, $L(-3, -3)$, $M(2, -2)$, $N(2, -1)$

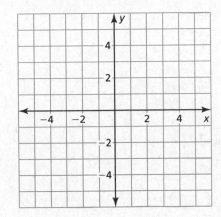

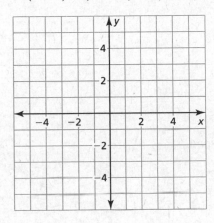

In Exercises 6–9, $k \parallel m$, $\overline{UV}$ is reflected in line k, and $\overline{U'V'}$ Is reflected in line m.

6. A translation maps $\overline{UV}$ onto which segment?

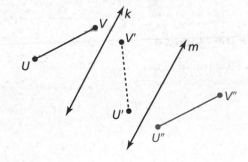

7. Which lines are perpendicular to $\overline{UU''}$?

8. Why is V'' the image of V? Explain your reasoning.

9. If the distance between k and m is 5 inches, what is the length of $\overline{VV''}$?

10. What is the angle of rotation that maps A onto A''?

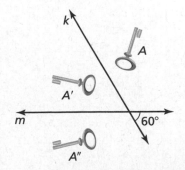

Chapter 12 Maintaining Mathematical Proficiency

Find the coordinates of the midpoint M of the segment with the given endpoints. Then find the distance between the two points.

1. $A(3, 1)$ and $B(5, 5)$

2. $F(0, -6)$ and $G(8, -4)$

3. $P(-2, -7)$ and $B(-4, 5)$

4. $S(10, -5)$ and $T(7, -9)$

Solve the equation.

5. $9x - 6 = 7x$

6. $2r + 6 = 5r - 9$

7. $20 - 3n = 2n + 30$

8. $8t - 5 = 6t - 4$

12.1 Angles of Triangles
For use with Exploration 12.1

Essential Question   How are the angle measures of a triangle related?

---

1   EXPLORATION: Writing a Conjecture

Go to *BigIdeasMath.com* for an interactive tool to investigate this exploration.

Work with a partner.

    a. Use dynamic geometry software to draw any triangle and label it $\triangle ABC$.

    b. Find the measures of the interior angles of the triangle.

    c. Find the sum of the interior angle measures.

    d. Repeat parts (a)–(c) with several other triangles. Then write a conjecture about the sum of the measures of the interior angles of a triangle.

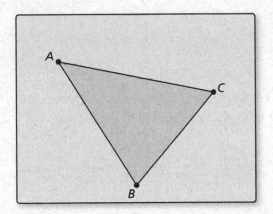

Sample
Angles
$m\angle A = 43.67°$
$m\angle B = 81.87°$
$m\angle C = 54.46°$

12.1 Angles of Triangles (continued)

2 **EXPLORATION:** Writing a Conjecture

Go to *BigIdeasMath.com* for an interactive tool to investigate this exploration.

Work with a partner.

a. Use dynamic geometry software to draw any triangle and label it △*ABC*.

b. Draw an exterior angle at any vertex and find its measure.

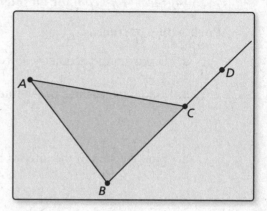

c. Find the measures of the two nonadjacent interior angles of the triangle.

Sample
Angles
$m\angle A = 43.67°$

d. Find the sum of the measures of the two nonadjacent interior angles. Compare this sum to the measure of the exterior angle.

$m\angle B = 81.87°$

$m\angle ACD = 125.54°$

e. Repeat parts (a)–(d) with several other triangles. Then write a conjecture that compares the measure of an exterior angle with the sum of the measures of the two nonadjacent interior angles.

Communicate Your Answer

3. How are the angle measures of a triangle related?

4. An exterior angle of a triangle measures 32°. What do you know about the measures of the interior angles? Explain your reasoning.

12.1 **Notetaking with Vocabulary**
For use after Lesson 12.1

In your own words, write the meaning of each vocabulary term.

interior angles

exterior angles

corollary to a theorem

Core Concepts

Classifying Triangles by Sides

Scalene Triangle	Isosceles Triangle	Equilateral Triangle

     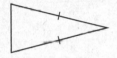

no congruent sides   at least 2 congruent sides   3 congruent sides

Classifying Triangles by Angles

Acute Triangle   Right Triangle   Obtuse Triangle   Equiangular Triangle

3 acute angles   1 right angle   1 obtuse angle   3 congruent angles

Notes:

12.1 Notetaking with Vocabulary (continued)

Theorems

Triangle Sum Theorem

The sum of the measures of the interior angles of a triangle is 180°.

Notes:

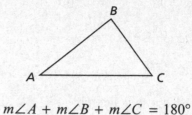

$$m\angle A + m\angle B + m\angle C = 180°$$

Exterior Angle Theorem

The measure of an exterior angle of a triangle is equal to the sum of the measures of the two nonadjacent interior angles.

Notes:

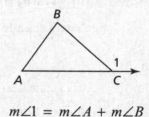

$$m\angle 1 = m\angle A + m\angle B$$

Corollary to the Triangle Sum Theorem

The acute angles of a right triangle are complementary.

Notes:

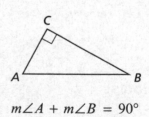

$$m\angle A + m\angle B = 90°$$

12.1 **Notetaking with Vocabulary** (continued)

Extra Practice

In Exercises 1–3, classify the triangle by its sides and by measuring its angles.

1.
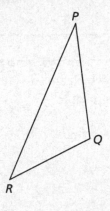

2.
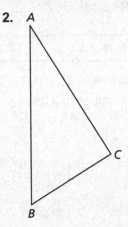

3.
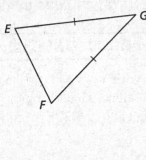

4. Classify △*ABC* by its sides. Then determine whether it is a right triangle.

$A(6, 6), B(9, 3), C(2, 2)$

In Exercises 5 and 6, find the measure of the exterior angle.

5.
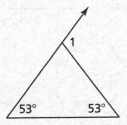

6.
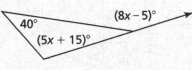

7. In a right triangle, the measure of one acute angle is twice the sum of the measure of the other acute angle and 30. Find the measure of each acute angle in the right triangle.

12.2 Congruent Polygons
For use with Exploration 12.2

Essential Question Given two congruent triangles, how can you use rigid motions to map one triangle to the other triangle?

1 EXPLORATION: Describing Rigid Motions

Work with a partner. Of the three transformations you studied in Chapter 11, which are rigid motions? Under a rigid motion, why is the image of a triangle always congruent to the original triangle? Explain you reasoning.

Translation   Reflection   Rotation

2 EXPLORATION: Finding a Composition of Rigid Motions

Go to *BigIdeasMath.com* for an interactive tool to investigate this exploration.

Work with a partner. Describe a composition of rigid motions that maps $\triangle ABC$ to $\triangle DEF$. Use dynamic geometry software to verify your answer.

    a. $\triangle ABC \cong \triangle DEF$ **b.** $\triangle ABC \cong \triangle DEF$

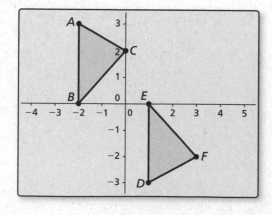 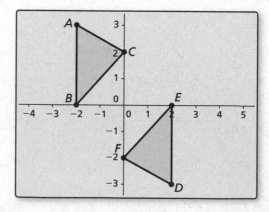

12.2 **Congruent Polygons** (continued)

2 **EXPLORATION:** Finding a Composition of Rigid Motions (continued)

c. $\triangle ABC \cong \triangle DEF$

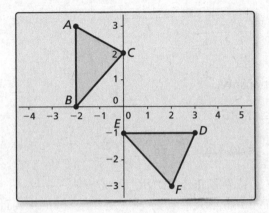

d. $\triangle ABC \cong \triangle DEF$

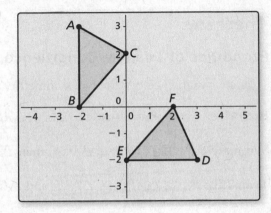

Communicate Your Answer

3. Given two congruent triangles, how can you use rigid motions to map one triangle to the other triangle?

4. The vertices of $\triangle ABC$ are $A(1, 1), B(3, 2),$ and $C(4, 4).$ The vertices of $\triangle DEF$ are $D(2, -1), E(0, 0),$ and $F(-1, 2).$ Describe a composition of rigid motions that maps $\triangle ABC$ to $\triangle DEF.$

12.2 Notetaking with Vocabulary
For use after Lesson 12.2

In your own words, write the meaning of each vocabulary term.

corresponding parts

Theorems

Properties of Triangle Congruence

Triangle congruence is reflexive, symmetric, and transitive.

Reflexive   For any triangle $\triangle ABC$, $\triangle ABC \cong \triangle ABC$.

Symmetric   If $\triangle ABC \cong \triangle DEF$, then $\triangle DEF \cong \triangle ABC$.

Transitive   If $\triangle ABC \cong \triangle DEF$ and $\triangle DEF \cong \triangle JKL$, then $\triangle ABC \cong \triangle JKL$.

Notes:

Third Angles Theorem

If two angles of one triangle are congruent to two angles of another triangle, then the third angles are also congruent.

Notes:

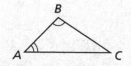
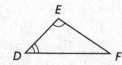

If $\angle A \cong \angle D$ and $\angle B \cong \angle E$, then $\angle C \cong \angle F$.

Name _____ Date _____

Extra Practice

In Exercises 1 and 2, identify all pairs of congruent corresponding parts. Then write another congruence statement for the polygons.

1. $\triangle PQR \cong \triangle STU$

2. $ABCD \cong EFGH$

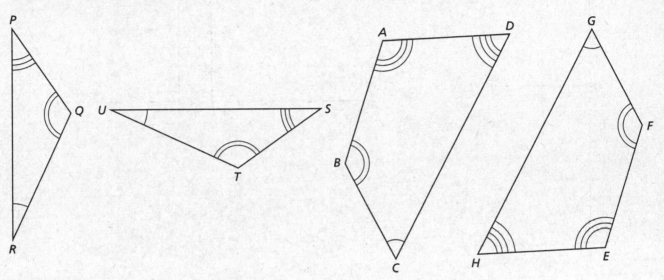

In Exercises 3 and 4, find the values of x and y.

3. $\triangle XYZ \cong \triangle RST$

4. $ABCD \cong EFGH$

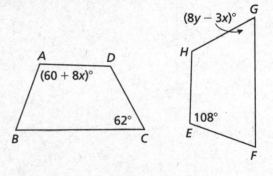

12.2 **Notetaking with Vocabulary** (continued)

In Exercises 5 and 6, show that the polygons are congruent. Explain your reasoning.

5.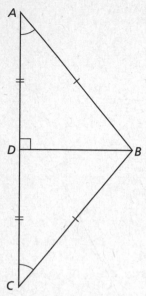

6.

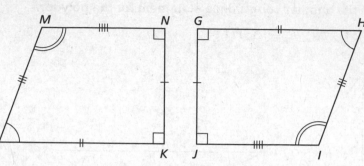

In Exercises 7 and 8, find $m\angle 1$.

7.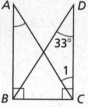

8.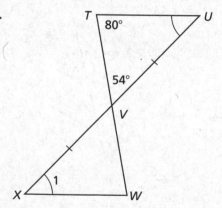

12.3 Proving Triangle Congruence by SAS
For use with Exploration 12.3

Essential Question What can you conclude about two triangles when you know that two pairs of corresponding sides and the corresponding included angles are congruent?

1 EXPLORATION: Drawing Triangles

Go to *BigIdeasMath.com* for an interactive tool to investigate this exploration.

Work with a partner. Use dynamic geometry software.

a. Construct circles with radii of 2 units and 3 units centered at the origin. Construct a 40° angle with its vertex at the origin. Label the vertex *A*.

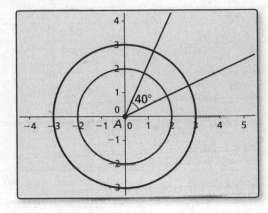

b. Locate the point where one ray of the angle intersects the smaller circle and label this point *B*. Locate the point where the other ray of the angle intersects the larger circle and label this point *C*. Then draw △*ABC*.

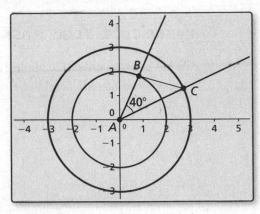

c. Find *BC*, *m∠B*, and *m∠C*.

d. Repeat parts (a)–(c) several times, redrawing the angle in different positions. Keep track of your results by completing the table on the next page. What can you conclude?

12.3 **Proving Triangle Congruence by SAS** (continued)

1 **EXPLORATION:** Drawing Triangles (continued)

	A	B	C	AB	AC	BC	m∠A	m∠B	m∠C
1.	(0, 0)			2	3		40°		
2.	(0, 0)			2	3		40°		
3.	(0, 0)			2	3		40°		
4.	(0, 0)			2	3		40°		
5.	(0, 0)			2	3		40°		

Communicate Your Answer

2. What can you conclude about two triangles when you know that two pairs of corresponding sides and the corresponding included angles are congruent?

3. How would you prove your conclusion in Exploration 1(d)?

12.3

Notetaking with Vocabulary
For use after Lesson 12.3

In your own words, write the meaning of each vocabulary term.

congruent figures

rigid motion

Theorems

Side-Angle-Side (SAS) Congruence Theorem

If two sides and the included angle of one triangle are congruent to two sides and the included angle of a second triangle, then the two triangles are congruent.

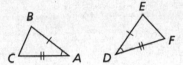

If $\overline{AB} \cong \overline{DE}, \angle A \cong \angle D$, and $\overline{AC} \cong \overline{DF}$, then $\triangle ABC \cong \triangle DEF$.

Notes:

12.3   Notetaking with Vocabulary (continued)

Extra Practice

In Exercises 1 and 2, write a proof.

1. **Given** $\overline{BD} \perp \overline{AC},\ \overline{AD} \cong \overline{CD}$

   Prove $\triangle ABD \cong \triangle CBD$

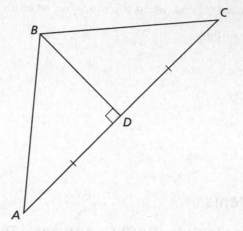

STATEMENTS	REASONS

2. **Given** $\overline{JN} \cong \overline{MN},\ \overline{NK} \cong \overline{NL}$

   Prove $\triangle JNK \cong \triangle MNL$

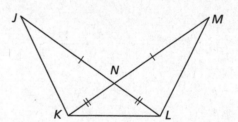

STATEMENTS	REASONS

12.3 **Notetaking with Vocabulary** (continued)

In Exercises 3 and 4, use the given information to name two triangles that are congruent. Explain your reasoning.

3. $\angle EPF \cong \angle GPH$, and P is the center of the circle.

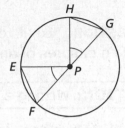

4. $ABCDEF$ is a regular hexagon.

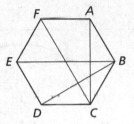

5. A quilt is made of triangles. You know $\overline{PS} \parallel \overline{QR}$ and $\overline{PS} \cong \overline{QR}$. Use the SAS Congruence Theorem to show that $\triangle PQR \cong \triangle RSP$.

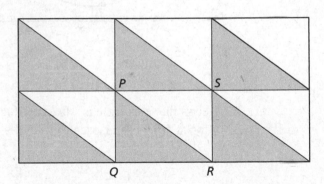

12.4 Equilateral and Isosceles Triangles
For use with Exploration 12.4

Essential Question What conjectures can you make about the side lengths and angle measures of an isosceles triangle?

---

1 **EXPLORATION: Writing a Conjecture about Isosceles Triangles**

Go to *BigIdeasMath.com* for an interactive tool to investigate this exploration.

Work with a partner. Use dynamic geometry software.

    a. Construct a circle with a radius of 3 units centered at the origin.

    b. Construct $\triangle ABC$ so that B and C are on the circle and A is at the origin.

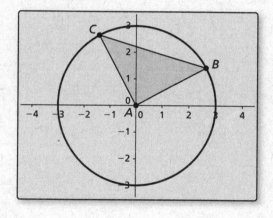

Sample
Points
$A(0, 0)$
$B(2.64, 1.42)$
$C(-1.42, 2.64)$
Segments
$AB = 3$
$AC = 3$
$BC = 4.24$
Angles
$m\angle A = 90°$
$m\angle B = 45°$
$m\angle C = 45°$

    c. Recall that a triangle is *isosceles* if it has at least two congruent sides. Explain why $\triangle ABC$ is an isosceles triangle.

    d. What do you observe about the angles of $\triangle ABC$?

    e. Repeat parts (a)–(d) with several other isosceles triangles using circles of different radii. Keep track of your observations by completing the table on the next page. Then write a conjecture about the angle measures of an isosceles triangle.

Name_____ Date_____

12.4 **Equilateral and Isosceles Triangles** (continued)

1 **EXPLORATION:** Writing a Conjecture about Isosceles Triangles (continued)

		A	B	C	AB	AC	BC	m∠A	m∠B	m∠C
Sample	**1.**	(0, 0)	(2.64, 1.42)	(−1.42, 2.64)	3	3	4.24	90°	45°	45°
	2.	(0, 0)								
	3.	(0, 0)								
	4.	(0, 0)								
	5.	(0, 0)								

    f. Write the converse of the conjecture you wrote in part (e). Is the converse true?

Communicate Your Answer

    2. What conjectures can you make about the side lengths and angle measures of an isosceles triangle?

    3. How would you prove your conclusion in Exploration 1(e)? in Exploration 1(f)?

Name _____ Date _____

In your own words, write the meaning of each vocabulary term.

legs

vertex angle

base

base angles

Theorems

Base Angles Theorem

If two sides of a triangle are congruent, then the angles opposite them are congruent.

If $\overline{AB} \cong \overline{AC}$, then $\angle B \cong \angle C$.

Converse of the Base Angles Theorem

If two angles of a triangle are congruent, then the sides opposite them are congruent.

If $\angle B \cong \angle C$, then $\overline{AB} \cong \overline{AC}$.

Notes:

12.4 Notetaking with Vocabulary (continued)

Corollaries

Corollary to the Base Angles Theorem

If a triangle is equilateral, then it is equiangular.

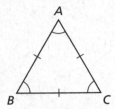

Corollary to the Converse of the Base Angles Theorem

If a triangle is equiangular, then it is equilateral.

Notes:

Extra Practice

In Exercises 1–4, complete the statement. State which theorem you used.

1. If $\overline{NJ} \cong \overline{NM}$, then $\angle$_____ $\cong \angle$_____.

2. If $\overline{LM} \cong \overline{LN}$, then $\angle$_____ $\cong \angle$_____.

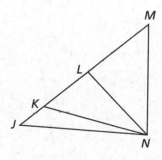

3. If $\angle NKM \cong \angle NMK$, then _____ $\cong$ _____.

4. If $\angle LJN \cong \angle LNJ$, then _____ $\cong$ _____.

12.4 **Notetaking with Vocabulary** (continued)

In Exercises 5 and 6, find the value of *x*.

5.

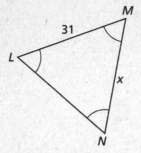

6.

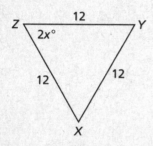

In Exercises 7 and 8, find the values of *x* and *y*.

7.

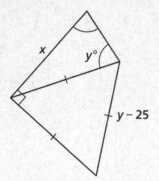

8.

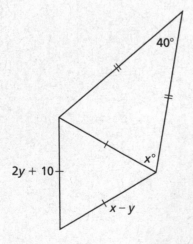

12.5 **Proving Triangle Congruence by SSS**
For use with Exploration 12.5

Essential Question What can you conclude about two triangles when you know the corresponding sides are congruent?

1 EXPLORATION: Drawing Triangles

Go to *BigIdeasMath.com* for an interactive tool to investigate this exploration.

Work with a partner. Use dynamic geometry software.

a. Construct circles with radii of 2 units and 3 units centered at the origin. Label the origin A. Then draw $\overline{BC}$ of length 4 units.

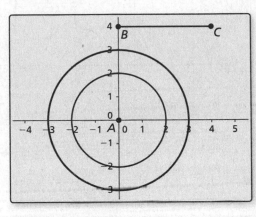

b. Move $\overline{BC}$ so that B is on the smaller circle and C is on the larger circle. Then draw $\triangle ABC$.

c. Explain why the side lengths of $\triangle ABC$ are 2, 3, and 4 units.

d. Find $m\angle A, m\angle B,$ and $m\angle C$.

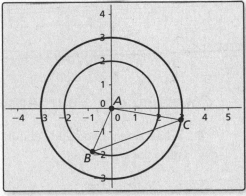

e. Repeat parts (b) and (d) several times, moving $\overline{BC}$ to different locations. Keep track of your results by completing the table on the next page. What can you conclude?

12.5 Proving Triangle Congruence by SSS (continued)

1 EXPLORATION: Drawing Triangles (continued)

	A	B	C	AB	AC	BC	m∠A	m∠B	m∠C
1.	(0, 0)			2	3	4			
2.	(0, 0)			2	3	4			
3.	(0, 0)			2	3	4			
4.	(0, 0)			2	3	4			
5.	(0, 0)			2	3	4			

Communicate Your Answer

2. What can you conclude about two triangles when you know the corresponding sides are congruent?

3. How would you prove your conclusion in Exploration 1(e)?

Notetaking with Vocabulary
For use after Lesson 12.5

In your own words, write the meaning of each vocabulary term.

legs

hypotenuse

Theorems

Side-Side-Side (SSS) Congruence Theorem

If three sides of one triangle are congruent to three sides of a second triangle, then the two triangles are congruent.

If $\overline{AB} \cong \overline{DE}$, $\overline{BC} \cong \overline{EF}$, and $\overline{AC} \cong \overline{DF}$, then $\triangle ABC \cong \triangle DEF$.

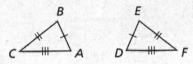

Notes:

Hypotenuse-Leg (HL) Congruence Theorem

If the hypotenuse and a leg of a right triangle are congruent to the hypotenuse and a leg of a second right triangle, then the two triangles are congruent.

If $\overline{AB} \cong \overline{DE}$, $\overline{AC} \cong \overline{DF}$, and $m\angle C = m\angle F = 90°$, then $\triangle ABC \cong \triangle DEF$.

Notes:

12.5 Notetaking with Vocabulary (continued)

Extra Practice

In Exercises 1–4, decide whether the congruence statement is true. Explain your reasoning.

1. $\triangle ABC \cong \triangle EDC$

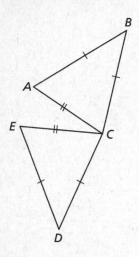

2. $\triangle KGH \cong \triangle HJK$

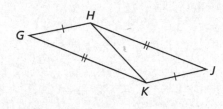

3. $\triangle UVW \cong \triangle XYZ$

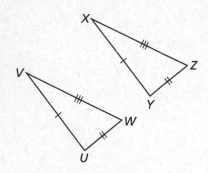

4. $\triangle RST \cong \triangle RPQ$

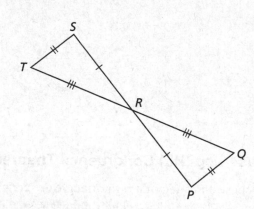

5. Determine whether the figure is stable. Explain your reasoning.

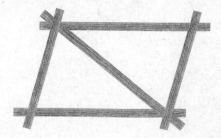

12.5 Notetaking with Vocabulary (continued)

6. Redraw the triangles so they are side by side with corresponding
   parts in the same position. Then write a proof.

Given B is the midpoint of $\overline{CD}$,
     $\overline{AB} \cong \overline{EB}$, $\angle C$ and $\angle D$ are right angles.

Prove $\triangle ABC \cong \triangle EBD$

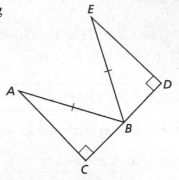

STATEMENTS	REASONS

7. Write a proof.

Given $\overline{IE} \cong \overline{EJ} \cong \overline{JL} \cong \overline{LH} \cong \overline{HK} \cong \overline{KI} \cong$
   $\overline{EK} \cong \overline{KF} \cong \overline{FH} \cong \overline{HG} \cong \overline{GL} \cong \overline{LE}$

Prove $\triangle EFG \cong \triangle HIJ$

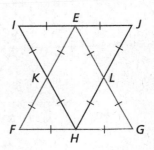

STATEMENTS	REASONS

12.6 Proving Triangle Congruence by ASA and AAS

For use with Exploration 12.6

Essential Question What information is sufficient to determine whether two triangles are congruent?

---

1 **EXPLORATION:** Determining Whether SSA Is Sufficient

Go to *BigIdeasMath.com* for an interactive tool to investigate this exploration.

Work with a partner.

   a. Use dynamic geometry software to construct $\triangle ABC$. Construct the triangle so that vertex B is at the origin, $\overline{AB}$ has a length of 3 units, and $\overline{BC}$ has a length of 2 units.

   b. Construct a circle with a radius of 2 units centered at the origin. Locate point D where the circle intersects $\overline{AC}$. Draw $\overline{BD}$.

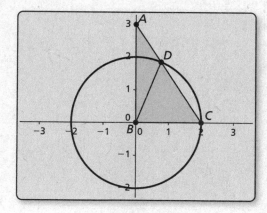

Sample
Points
$A(0, 3)$
$B(0, 0)$
$C(2, 0)$
$D(0.77, 1.85)$
Segments
$AB = 3$
$AC = 3.61$
$BC = 2$
$AD = 1.38$
Angle
$m\angle A = 33.69°$

   c. $\triangle ABC$ and $\triangle ABD$ have two congruent sides and a nonincluded congruent angle. Name them.

   d. Is $\triangle ABC \cong \triangle ABD$? Explain your reasoning.

   e. Is SSA sufficient to determine whether two triangles are congruent? Explain your reasoning.

12.6 Proving Triangle Congruence by ASA and AAS (continued)

---

2 EXPLORATION: Determining Valid Congruence Theorems

Go to *BigIdeasMath.com* for an interactive tool to investigate this exploration.

Work with a partner. Use dynamic geometry software to determine which of the following are valid triangle congruence theorems. For those that are not valid, write a counterexample. Explain your reasoning.

Possible Congruence Theorem	Valid or not valid?
SSS	
SSA	
SAS	
AAS	
ASA	
AAA	

Communicate Your Answer

3. What information is sufficient to determine whether two triangles are congruent?

4. Is it possible to show that two triangles are congruent using more than one congruence theorem? If so, give an example.

12.6 Notetaking with Vocabulary
For use after Lesson 12.6

In your own words, write the meaning of each vocabulary term.

congruent figures

rigid motion

Theorems

Angle-Side-Angle (ASA) Congruence Theorem

If two angles and the included side of one triangle are congruent
to two angles and the included side of a second triangle, then the
two triangles are congruent.

If $\angle A \cong \angle D$, $\overline{AC} \cong \overline{DF}$, and $\angle C \cong \angle F$, then
$\triangle ABC \cong \triangle DEF$.

Notes:

Angle-Angle-Side (AAS) Congruence Theorem

If two angles and a non-included side of one triangle are
congruent to two angles and the corresponding non-included side
of a second triangle, then the two triangles are congruent.

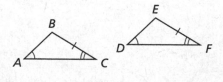

If $\angle A \cong \angle D$, $\angle C \cong \angle F$, and $\overline{BC} \cong \overline{EF}$, then
$\triangle ABC \cong \triangle DEF$.

Notes:

（Name）_____ Date _____

12.6 **Notetaking with Vocabulary** (continued)

Extra Practice

In Exercises 1–4, decide whether enough information is given to prove that the triangles are congruent. If so, state the theorem you would use.

1. $\triangle GHK, \triangle JKH$

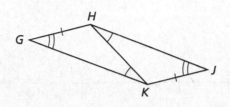

2. $\triangle ABC, \triangle DEC$

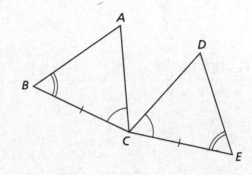

3. $\triangle JKL, \triangle MLK$

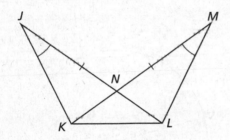

4. $\triangle RST, \triangle UVW$

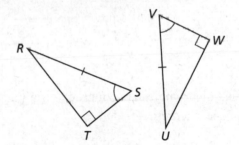

In Exercises 5 and 6, decide whether you can use the given information to prove that $\triangle LMN \cong \triangle PQR$. Explain your reasoning.

5. $\angle M \cong \angle Q, \angle N \cong \angle R, \overline{NL} \cong \overline{RP}$

6. $\angle L \cong \angle R, \angle M \cong \angle Q, \overline{LM} \cong \overline{PQ}$

12.6 **Notetaking with Vocabulary** (continued)

7. Prove that the triangles are congruent using the ASA Congruence Theorem.

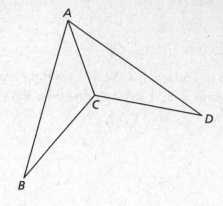

Given $\overline{AC}$ bisects $\angle DAB$ and $\angle DCB$.

Prove $\triangle ABC \cong \triangle ADC$

STATEMENTS	REASONS

8. Prove that the triangles are congruent using the AAS Congruence Theorem.

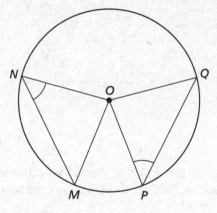

Given O is the center of the circle and $\angle N \cong \angle P$.

Prove $\triangle MNO \cong \triangle PQO$

STATEMENTS	REASONS

12.7 **Using Congruent Triangles**
For use with Exploration 12.7

Essential Question   How can you use congruent triangles to make an indirect measurement?

1 **EXPLORATION: Measuring the Width of a River**

Work with a partner. The figure shows how a surveyor can measure the width of a river by making measurements on only one side of the river.

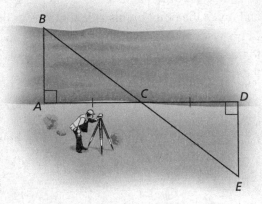

a. Study the figure. Then explain how the surveyor can find the width of the river.

b. Write a proof to verify that the method you described in part (a) is valid.

Given $\angle A$ is a right angle, $\angle D$ is a right angle, $\overline{AC} \cong \overline{CD}$

c. Exchange proofs with your partner and discuss the reasoning used.

12.7 Using Congruent Triangles (continued)

2 EXPLORATION: Measuring the Width of a River

Work with a partner. It was reported that one of Napoleon's officers estimated the width of a river as follows. The officer stood on the bank of the river and lowered the visor on his cap until the farthest thing visible was the edge of the bank on the other side. He then turned and noted the point on his side that was in line with the tip of his visor and his eye. The officer then paced the distance to this point and concluded that distance was the width of the river.

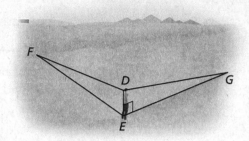

    a. Study the figure. Then explain how the officer concluded that the width of the river is *EG*.

    b. Write a proof to verify that the conclusion the officer made is correct.

       Given   ∠*DEG* is a right angle, ∠*DEF* is a right angle, ∠*EDG* ≅ ∠*EDF*

    c. Exchange proofs with your partner and discuss the reasoning used.

Communicate Your Answer

    3. How can you use congruent triangles to make an indirect measurement?

    4. Why do you think the types of measurements described in Explorations 1 and 2 are called *indirect* measurements?

Name____ Date__________

12.7 Notetaking with Vocabulary
For use after Lesson 12.7

In your own words, write the meaning of each vocabulary term.

congruent figures

corresponding parts

construction

perpendicular lines

Notes:

12.7 Notetaking with Vocabulary (continued)

Extra Practice

In Exercises 1–3, explain how to prove that the statement is true.

1. $\overline{UV} \cong \overline{XV}$

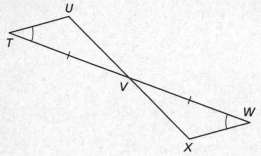

2. $\overline{TS} \cong \overline{VR}$

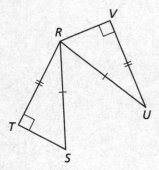

3. $\angle JLK \cong \angle MLN$

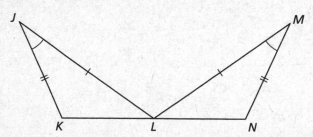

In Exercises 4 and 5, write a plan to prove that $\angle 1 \cong \angle 2$.

4.

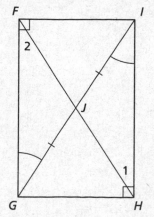

12.7 **Notetaking with Vocabulary** (continued)

5.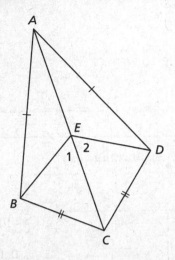

6. Write a proof to verify that the construction is valid.

Ray bisects an angle

Plan for Proof Show that $\triangle ABD \cong \triangle ACD$ by the SSS Congruence Theorem. Use corresponding parts of congruent triangles to show that $\angle BAD \cong \angle CAD$.

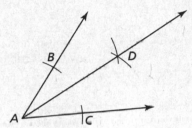

STATEMENTS	REASONS

12.8 Coordinate Proofs
For use with Exploration 12.8

Essential Question How can you use a coordinate plane to write a proof?

1 EXPLORATION: Writing a Coordinate Proof

Go to *BigIdeasMath.com* for an interactive tool to investigate this exploration.

Work with a partner.

a. Use dynamic geometry software to draw $\overline{AB}$ with endpoints $A(0, 0)$ and $B(6, 0)$.

b. Draw the vertical line $x = 3$.

c. Draw $\triangle ABC$ so that C lies on the line $x = 3$.

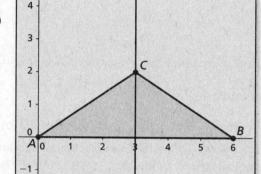

Sample
Points
$A(0, 0)$
$B(6, 0)$
$C(3, y)$
Segments
$AB = 6$
Line
$x = 3$

d. Use your drawing to prove that $\triangle ABC$ is an isosceles triangle.

2 EXPLORATION: Writing a Coordinate Proof

Go to *BigIdeasMath.com* for an interactive tool to investigate this exploration.

Work with a partner.

a. Use dynamic geometry software to draw $\overline{AB}$ with endpoints $A(0, 0)$ and $B(6, 0)$.

b. Draw the vertical line $x = 3$.

c. Plot the point $C(3, 3)$ and draw $\triangle ABC$. Then use your drawing to prove that $\triangle ABC$ is an isosceles right triangle.

12.8   **Coordinate Proofs** (continued)

---

2   **EXPLORATION:** Writing a Coordinate Proof (continued)

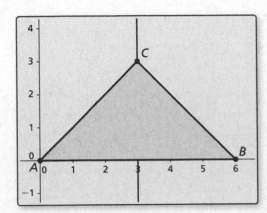

Sample
Points
$A(0, 0)$
$B(6, 0)$
$C(3, 3)$
Segments
  $AB = 6$
  $BC = 4.24$
  $AC = 4.24$
Line
  $x = 3$

  d. Change the coordinates of C so that C lies below the x-axis and $\triangle ABC$ is an isosceles right triangle.

  e. Write a coordinate proof to show that if C lies on the line $x = 3$ and $\triangle ABC$ is an isosceles right triangle, then C must be the point $(3, 3)$ or the point found in part (d).

Communicate Your Answer

  3. How can you use a coordinate plane to write a proof?

  4. Write a coordinate proof to prove that $\triangle ABC$ with vertices $A(0, 0)$, $B(6, 0)$, and $C\left(3, 3\sqrt{3}\right)$ is an equilateral triangle.

12.8 Notetaking with Vocabulary
For use after Lesson 12.8

In your own words, write the meaning of each vocabulary term.

coordinate proof

Notes:

12.8 Notetaking with Vocabulary (continued)

Extra Practice

In Exercises 1 and 2, place the figure in a coordinate plane in a convenient way. Assign coordinates to each vertex. Explain the advantages of your placement.

1. an obtuse triangle with height of 3 units and base of 2 units

2. a rectangle with length of $2w$

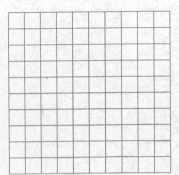

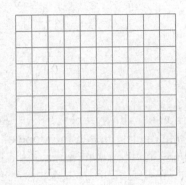

In Exercises 3 and 4, write a plan for the proof.

3. **Given**   Coordinates of vertices of $\triangle OPR$ and $\triangle QRP$

     Proof $\triangle OPR \cong \triangle QRP$

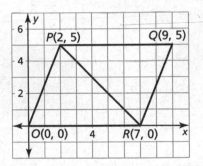

12.8 **Notetaking with Vocabulary** (continued)

4. **Given** Coordinates of vertices of $\triangle OAB$ and $\triangle CDB$

    Prove B is the midpoint of $\overline{AD}$ and $\overline{OC}$.

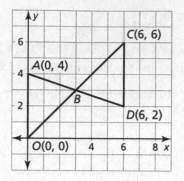

5. Graph the triangle with vertices $A(0, 0)$, $B(3m, m)$, and $C(0, 3m)$. Find the length and the slope of each side of the triangle. Then find the coordinates of the midpoint of each side. Is the triangle a right triangle? isosceles? Explain. (Assume all variables are positive.)

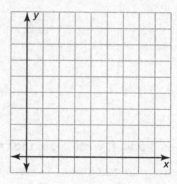

6. Write a coordinate proof.

    Given Coordinates of vertices of $\triangle OEF$ and $\triangle OGF$

    Prove $\triangle OEF \cong \triangle OGF$

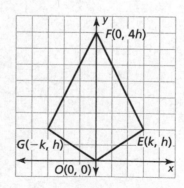